LEARNING DISABILITIES

LEARNING DISABILITIES

A Book of Readings

Compiled and Edited by

LARRY A. FAAS

Associate Professor of Special Education
Arizona State University
Tempe, Arizona

CHARLES C THOMAS • PUBLISHER
Springfield • Illinois • U.S.A.

Published and Distributed Throughout the World by
CHARLES C THOMAS • PUBLISHER
Bannerstone House
301-327 East Lawrence Avenue, Springfield, Illinois, U.S.A.

© *1972, by* CHARLES C THOMAS • PUBLISHER
ISBN 0-398-02276-3
Library of Congress Catalog Card Number: 73-187651

Printed in the United States of America
Q-1

CONTRIBUTORS

ALEX BANNATYNE

Director, Bannatyne Children's Learning Center
Miami, Florida

RAY H. BARSCH

Educational Consultant
Canoga Park, California

BARBARA BATEMAN

Professor of Education
University of Oregon
Eugene, Oregon

FRANCIS X. BLAIR

Director, Laboratory School for Exceptional Children
University of Wisconsin—Milwaukee
Milwaukee, Wisconsin

JOHN E. BOLEN

Dean, School of Education
Wisconsin State University
Stevens Point, Wisconsin

GEORGE H. EARLY

Clinical Director
Achievement Center for Children
Purdue University
Lafayette, Indiana

RUTH EDGINGTON

Education Specialist
Child Study Center
University of Arkansas Medical Center
Little Rock, Arkansas

NATHAN FLAX

Director of Vision Training Department
The Optometric Center of New York
New York City, New York

MARYBETH P. FREY

Primary Level Teacher
Plesantdale School
La Grange, Illinois

JERRY GIBSON

Assistant Director
Educational Placement
University of Southern California
Los Angeles, California

BERNICE V. GUNDERSON

Language Arts Education
Southwestern Minnesota State College
Marshall, Minnesota

R. G. HECKELMAN

Coordinator Pupil Personnel Services
Lucia Mar Unified School District
Pesino Beach, California

RONALD S. HOROWITZ

Mathematics Teacher
Princeton Regional Schools
Princeton, New Jersey

DORIS J. JOHNSON

Institute for Language Disorders
Northwestern University
Evanston, Illinois

CORRINE E. KASS

Associate Professor
University of Arizona
Tucson, Arizona

NEWELL C. KEPHART

Glen Haven Achievement Center
Fort Collins, Colorado

MADELEINE LASSERS

San Francisco City College
San Francisco, California

SHIRLEY LINN

Learning Disabilities Teacher
Topeka Public Schools
Topeka, Kansas

MIRIAM SPER MAGDOL

Learning Disabilities Teacher
Rochester, New York

GORDON H. NAYLOR

Director of Guidance
Hacienda La Puente Unified School District
La Puente, California

JAY M. ROTHBERG

Associate Director
New England Special Education
Instructional Materials Center
Boston University
Boston, Massachusetts

EDWARD G. SCAGLIOTTA

Director, The Midland School
North Branch, New Jersey

IRVING L. SHAPIRO

Optometrist Specializing in Developmental Vision
Tonawanda, New York

THEODORE M. SHARPE

Psychology Intern
University of Florida
Gainesville, Florida

JUDITH A. WEINTHALER

Educational Diagnostician
Brookline Public Schools
Brookline, Massachusetts

PREFACE

T HE RAPID GROWTH of today's universities and their programs for the preparation of teachers of learning disabled children has made assigned library readings impractical if not totally impossible on many campuses. When the large number of students enrolled in a preparation program all attempt to gain access to a single reading, the futility of their efforts becomes obvious. These class assignments often tie up large amounts of significant literature, making it difficult for individual students who wish to conduct research.

The readings in this book are selected to provide the reader with an overview of educational services provided for children in our schools who have learning disabilities. This book will be useful not only to the university student preparing to teach the learning disabled child, but to the school administrator, school psychologist, school social worker, elementary school counselor, and the teacher of learning disabled children as well.

Sections A and B focus upon the definition, characteristics and identification of learning disabilities.

Perceptual-motor disabilities, visual-perceptual disabilities and auditory perceptual and communication disorders are considered in Sections C, D and E.

The book's concluding sections concentrate upon disabilities in the basic skill areas, programming for effective remediation and parent counseling.

I would like to extend my thanks to the authors, editors, and publishers who granted permission to reprint their work in this volume. I am especially appreciative of the efforts of Sue Lincoln Waters, Becky Busboom, and Beverly Krehbiel, who assisted me in the preparation of the final manuscript. Particular gratitude is expressed to my wife, Patricia, for her critical evaluation and assistance.

LARRY A. FAAS

CONTENTS

SECTION A

INTRODUCTION, DEFINITIONS AND CHARACTERISTICS

Chapter

SECTION B

IDENTIFICATION

SECTION C

PERCEPTUAL-MOTOR DISABILITIES

SECTION D

VISUAL-PERCEPTUAL DISABILITIES

SECTION E

AUDITORY-PERCEPTUAL AND COMMUNICATION DISABILITIES

SECTION F

BASIC SKILL DEFICITS

SECTION G

PROGRAMMING FOR EFFECTIVE
REMEDIATION

SECTION H

PARENT COUNSELING

LEARNING DISABILITIES

SECTION A

INTRODUCTION, DEFINITIONS
AND CHARACTERISTICS

Chapter 1

INTRODUCTION TO LEARNING DISABILITIES

CORRINE E. KASS

T HE EFFECTS OF CONTINUING FAILURE on the human being, especially when it is recognized by the person himself, has been well
documented in psychiatry, psychology, and educational psychology. The phenomenon of failure in learning disabilities is
well known. The child who is not achieving as expected is
frustrated and is puzzling to those adults responsible for his welfare. Experts from a number of disciplines are increasingly
reaching a consensus regarding the antidote to failure: successful
learning. Educational management then becomes paramount in
importance, with ancillary aids given when necessary by the
medical and mental health professions.

Basic to an understanding of the area of learning disabilities
within special education are several assumptions: (1) There are
children with a handicapping condition who can be so labeled.
(2) Although services for these children are scarce now, both
public and private programs are growing in numbers. (3) While
the understanding of learning disabilities is complex, behavioral
science research indicates that the child with learning disabilities
has psychological process deficits and the usual educational
manipulation of the environment is not adequate for remediation
purposes. (4) The handicapping condition known as learning
disabilities can be diagnosed educationally and psychologically
and specialized remedial education programs can be prescribed.

Reprinted from *Seminars In Psychiatry*, Vol. 1, No. 3 (August, 1969). By permission of the author and Henry M. Stratton, Inc., publisher.

LABELING

The question of labeling generally precedes definition. Special educators have been going through a period of transition regarding labeling children according to the traditional categories. In their efforts to revise and improve, many have snatched at the term learning disabilities as a catchall educational phrase to liberate special education from medical models. After all, who can deny that all handicapped children have problems of learning in normal ways? By casting categories aside, some have felt it would be possible to group children wtih varying handicaps together with a "generalist" special educator. While this view has not gained widespread approval among special educators, it has served to improve communication among the category specialists and will undoubtedly lead to improved services for all children with handicaps.

In contrast to special education's attempt to erase category lines is the general public's propensity for creating labels. It is amazing with what alacrity laymen and professionals alike have applied such labels as "dyslexia," "minimal brain dysfunction," "interjacent child," "hyperkinetic child," "brain-injured," "invisibly crippled," and "shadow children" without having more than a superficial list of characteristics, all of which can probably be found to some extent within the normal population. As a result, labels become misused. "Learning disabilities," as a label, is also being misused rather generally. Under the Federal Elementary and Secondary Education Act, money is available for supplementary services to school children. Many of these projects use the term learning disabilities to refer to behavioral, social, and achievement problems with only vague reference to treatment services.

DEFINITION

The responsibility for the definition of a word lies with the labeler. I believe it is safe to say that in no other area of special education has so much effort and controversy gone into the refinement of a definition which would characterize those children who come within the responsibility of special education and require special methods and techniques. Over time, definitions have evolved through the efforts of various groups. Following are five such definitions given in chronological order.

1. (1962) The following definition appeared in a textbook on exceptional children:

> A learning disability refers to a retardation, disorder, or delayed development in one or more of the processes of speech, language, reading, spelling, writing, or arithmetic resulting from a possible cerebral dysfunction and/or emotional or behavioral disturbance and not from mental retardation, sensory deprivation, or cultural or instructional factors.[5]

2. (1966) A task force on terminology and identification of the "child with minimal brain dysfunction" was co-sponsored by the National Society for Crippled Children and Adults, Inc., and the National Institute of Neurological Diseases and Blindness of the National Institutes of Health.

> The term "minimal brain dysfunction syndrome" refers to children of near average, average, or above average general intelligence with certain learning or behavioral disabilities ranging from mild to severe, which are associated with deviations of function of the central nervous system. These deviations may manifest themselves by various combinations of impairment in perception, conceptualization, language, memory, and control of attention, impulse, or motor function.
>
> Similar symptoms may or may not complicate the problems of children with cerebral palsy, epilepsy, mental retardation, blindness, or deafness.[7]

3. (1967) At the 1967 conference, the Association for Children with Learning Disabilities, a national parent organization, adopted the following definition formulated by professionals and a group of executives of the organization:

> A child with learning disabilities is one with adequate mental ability, sensory processes, and emotional stability who has a limited number of specific deficits in perceptual, integrative, or expressive processes which severely impair learning efficiency. This includes children who have central nervous system dysfunction which is expressed primarily in impaired learning efficiency.[1]

4. (1967) A further clarification of learning disabilities for the educator was suggested at an Institute for Advanced Study which

was planned collaboratively by Northwestern University (Institute for Language Disabilities) and the Unit on Learning Disabilities Division of Training Programs, Bureau of Education for Handicapped, U. S. Office of Education. This meeting took place in August 1967, at Northwestern University. The fifteen invited special educators agreed on the following definition:

> A learning disability refers to one or more significant deficits in essential learning processes requiring special educational techniques for its remediation.
>
> Children with learning disability generally demonstrate a discrepancy between expected and actual achievement in one or more areas, such as spoken, reading, or written language, mathematics, and spatial orientation.
>
> The learning disability referred to is not primarily the result of sensory, motor, intellectual, or emotional handicap, or lack of opportunity to learn.
>
> Deficits are to be defined in terms of accepted diagnostic procedures in education and psychology.
>
> Essential learning processes are those currently referred to in behavioral science as perception, integration, and expression, either verbal or nonverbal.
>
> Special education techniques for remediation require educational planning based on the diagnostic procedures and findings.[5]

5. (1968) The National Advisory Committee to the Bureau of Education for the Handicapped, Office of Education, provided the following definition as a guideline to the Office of Education for its present program:

> Children with special learning disabilities exhibit a disorder in one or more of the basic psychological processes involved in understanding or in using spoken or written language. These may be manifested in disorders of listening, thinking, talking, reading, writing, spelling, or arithmetic. They include conditions which have been referred to as perceptual handicaps, brain injury, minimal brain dysfunction, dyslexia, developmental aphasia, etc. They do not include learning problems which are due primarily to visual, hearing, or motor handicaps, to mental retardation, emotional disturbance or to environmental deprivation.[6]

SERVICES AND PERSONNEL

Educational services for children with learning disabilities run the gamut from itinerant tutoring through resource rooms to special classes. In reality, education can be no better than the personnel providing the services, and marketable skills in the specialty of learning disabilities are extremely important. Several institutions of higher learning are presently engaged in guiding graduate students in their acquisition of specialized skills and knowledges. For a description of some of these programs, the reader is referred to Kass and Chalfant.[4]

The following skills and knowledges gained from a program in learning disabilities is submitted as a portrait of the special education "specialist."

The specialist will have a basic foundation or introduction to both the behavioral and physical sciences, with grounding in the humanities. This is generally accomplished in the first two years of a college education. Basic information regarding sensory functioning, classic research in perception from both the physiological and psychological areas, and experience with communication through the written word are steps toward becoming well educated in learning disabilities.

The specialist will acquire advanced knowledge at the graduate level as new discoveries are made concerning human learning. The neural basis of memory, for example, is constantly being clarified as research progresses. The student of learning disabilities learns to interpret and utilize information from discoveries about other facets of human learning as well as memory.

The specialist will be skilled in diagnosis and remediation of process deficits within the child. Testing skills require the incorporation of the principles of individual testing and the technical mastery of testing procedures. Remediation skills require understanding the deficits revealed by tests, and mastery of the application of appropriate pedagogy. The gap between diagnosis and remediation can be bridged through the *understanding* of learning deficits. One understanding of the specialist is the distinction among developmental, corrective, and specialized teaching. Developmental learning occurs in the majority of the population when environmental conditions and psychological characteristics follow the normal growth patterns. Corrective teaching is necessary when there has been a gap in a child's education due to such factors as absence from school. Specialized teaching is remedial instruction, which is defined by English and English[2] as "teaching that is designed to remove, where possible, specific causes of lack or deficiency." Corrective teaching can be given by the child's regular teacher with information about the level of achievement. Specialized teaching must be given by specialists trained in the diagnosis and remediation of learning disabilities. A programmed sequence by itself is not a remedial program.

The specialist will have practicum or internship experiences before having specialist status. At the present time, graduate students in learning disabilities enter the field from a variety of backgrounds. This factor has revealed identification problems. Students come from positions in remedial reading, elementary education, psychology, counseling, and special education. The programs in learning disabilities are located within departments of special education. During their practicum experiences, graduate students must find identity within the entire area of special education, as well as within the category of learning disabilities. The number of specialists in the category of learning disabilities is relatively small at the present time. Qualifications and professional standards have yet to be established on a nation-wide basis. Practicum experiences range from private settings to public school programs. Some hospital or institutional settings may also be used. The university center seems most reasonable during the identification transition. The university staff in learning disabilities provides the most rapid identification with the concept of the learning disability specialist.

The specialist will be able to work with an interdisciplinary team. With the characteristics listed above, the graduate of a learning disability program would be confident of the data he would carry to an evaluation team and thus would inspire the confidence shown in a professional who is an expert. A feeling of security about one's own expertise reflects itself in more effective team problem-solving.

The specialist will be able to carry out research. The research in learning disabilities appears to be in a transitional stage.[3] Students at the doctoral level in learning disabilities are expected to evaluate this transition and to help formulate imaginative research questions and methodology.

The specialist will be able to communicate with teachers. Consultants are to be found in the schools in increasing numbers. Over the years, the professional consultants who could not or would not communicate with teachers produced reports which were ignored. One of the major objectives for children with learning disabilities is to leave them in the regular classroom, if possible, while giving individualized tutoring, or to return them to the regular classroom as soon as possible. This means that the teacher must know what the child's learning disabilities are, what the specialist is doing about the disabilities, and what her role is to be in transferring remediated skills to everyday learning.

The specialist will develop a personal philosophy or structure as the basis of specialist status. With the explosion of knowledge in all disciplines, much confusion can result from a vague eclectic approach to learning disabilities. A structure encompasses the major factors in the human organism which relate to learning disabilities. The student will find such structures or theories in the literature and, through scholarship and synthesis, will incorporate and develop existing theories into expanding and more valid structures. The behavioral science procedures for the analysis of input-feedback-output processes may be the place to begin.

CONCLUSION

An introduction to learning disabilities, of necessity, begins with the label itself. No one profession has a premium on a label, however, and the use of a label without a definition is professional irresponsibility. In this paper, both labeling and definitions were considered. Professional training programs in the area of learning disabilities can be found throughout the country. A portrait of the specialist who graduates from such programs was presented. The challenge of the field of learning disabilities is enhanced by the pressure for services from both parents and professionals.

REFERENCES

1. Association for Children with Learning Disabilities. Annual conference, New York City, meeting of executives of the organization and selected professionals, 1967.
2. English, H. B., and English, A. C.: *A Comprehensive Dictionary of Psychological and Psychoanalytical Terms.* New York, McKay, 1958.

3. Kass, C. E.: Learning disabilities. *Rev Educ Res*, February 1969.
4. Kass, C. E., and Chalfant, J.: Training specialists for children with learning disabilities. In Hellmuth, J. (Ed.): *Learning Disorders.* Seattle, Special Child, 1968, Vol. 3.
5. Kirk, S. A.: *Educating Exceptional Children.* Boston, Houghton Mifflin, 1962, p. 263.
6. National Advisory Committee on Handicapped Children. First Annual Report, *Special Education for Handicapped Children.* Washington, U.S. Dept. HEW Office of Education, 1968.
7. National Society for Crippled Children and Adults, Inc., and the National Institute of Neurological Diseases and Blindness, of the National Institutes of Health. *Minimal Brain Dysfunction in Children.* Washington, U.S. Dept. of HEW, NINDB Monograph 3, 1966.
8. Northwestern University and U. S. Office of Education. Unpublished proceedings of the Conference on Learning Disabilities and Interrelated Handicaps. Evanston, August 8, 1967.

Chapter 2

VIEWPOINT: TEACHER OF THE NH CLASS

JERRY GIBSON

It is hoped that within a few years the neurologically handicapped (NH) child will be as widely recognized as the cerebral palsied and the mentally retarded child. Although the NH child's handicap is not as obvious or extreme, his disorder is serious and his teacher should be aware of the conditions which may be hindering his achievement. Briefly, the following are some of the conditions which have been noted in NH children to varying degrees:

1. Visual perception. Often NH children are not able to perceive complete objects. In viewing an object, one of its parts may come into the foreground, reducing the other parts to background status.

2. Auditory perception. Sometimes upon examination, NH children with suspected hearing loss are discovered to have auditory acuity intact. Auditory difficulty may then be considered a functional consequence of other psychological disturbances. NH children may be weak in pitch discrimination or tonal perception with obscurity of meaning.

3. Behavior. Often the NH child is overly active. He is unable to filter out the unimportant details of what he sees, hears, and feels, and often is unable to control his response to these stimuli.

4. Attention. Although the NH child may appear to be inattentive, he is actually *too* attentive—to everything. He is unable to rule out unessential stimuli; he is very sensitive to a great variety of stimuli. Thus, what appears to be inattention is really preoccupation with many unrelated and unessential details.

Reprinted from the *Journal Of The California Optometric Association*, January, 1966, pp. 34-41. By permission of the author and publisher.

5. Perseveration. Not able to readily integrate stimuli, the NH child is reluctant to let go of a situation that he has structured and continues to respond when the stimulus of his structured response is no longer present.

6. Posture. NH children frequently lack in precision of manipulation and movement. Some of them often bump into things because of their inability to judge size, shape, and distance.

7. Destructiveness. If the NH child does not see or hear as a normal child and is awkward, he is less able to take care of objects. Thus, his destructiveness is related in part to his visual, auditory, and motor problems.

8. Social competence. How can a child displaying the above conditions be accepted by his peers? Nonacceptance hinders his development in social experiences, which the NH child especially needs, and is partially responsible for subnormality in this area.

9. Retention. The NH child forgets easily, particularly in areas of abstract learning. Sometimes he displays surprising memory of concrete specific parts of a much earlier experience.

10. Laterality. Mixed dominance is often found in NH children, but authorities disagree as to the importance of these findings.

An important thing to remember is that not *all* NH children exhibit *all* of these traits. There is wide variation in the degree and number of characteristics evidenced. Considering these and their resultant problems makes obvious the importance of choosing a teacher for a special NH class with great care and thought. Many factors must be considered in this selection. A teacher of neurologically handicapped children should

1. Have considerable training in the psychological and physical development of children.

2. Have some preparation in the theory of NH education and in the use of specified materials and methods of classroom management.

3. Be able to establish a well organized program in which the children clearly know what is expected of them.

4. Be able to appraise individual needs and determine appropriate instructional levels quickly without creating anxiety in the children.

5. Fully accept and respect each child in his class.

6. Be interested in the unresolved problems of learning.

7. Be flexible, be able to experiment, possess initiative, ingenuity and sound judgment.

8. Be willing to stay with the same group of children for at least two years.

9. Devote as much time as possible during the first year to visiting and working with parents.

10. Develop an awareness of symptoms that are indicative of handicaps since the NH child is often multihandicapped and symptoms of one condition may actually be caused by a related handicap.

These conditions in selecting and keeping a teacher are impossible to achieve without the school district accepting some responsibilities in regard to the teacher. If an NH program is to be completely successful, it must be a united effort. Administrators and teachers of regular classes must be well informed as to the purpose and goals of the NH class. If possible, the district should provide a teacher assistant, one for every two classes. The responsibilities of this assistant would be (1) keeping records, (2) preparing teaching materials, (3) observing, (4) operating audio-visual equipment, and (5) providing relief for the teacher. The teacher should have a high degree of security, and the full cooperation and support of administrators and guidance department. He should be completely free of curricular responsibilities other than those specifically related to his NH class. Preferably, NH class enrollment should include eight children, with a maximum of ten.

The responsibility of the teacher, school, and parents of the NH child can be summed up in the question, *"Have we done all we can for this child?"* The fact that the NH child's development and learning processes have been altered by his handicap clearly indicates the need for modification of usual instructional procedures. The following discussion of an NH class shows this.

The NH class starts with one or two neurologically handicapped children, gradually increasing to a maximum of ten. Every possible unessential stimulus has been removed from the classroom or reduced in its visual, auditory, or tactual impressiveness. This gives the hyperactive and/or distractable child an increased opportunity to attend to those stimuli which are essential to his learning. This is best accomplished by each child having his own "office" work stall with the desk facing a blank wall, and no pictures or bulletin board displays in the room. The child is led to understand that since he is easily disturbed, he will be less affected if he works in his "office." He will like the "office" arrangement if he is made to feel provided for instead of banished.

The day begins with quiet, well structured activity which usually helps the NH child get off on the right foot. I have found great success in beginning with prepared arithmetic assignments for each child or easy review seat work. If a sharing period is planned, it is scheduled for the end of the day instead of the beginning.

Since the NH child often needs to be reinforced with a reminder of what is expected of him, the teacher frequently discusses what is expected with the class. The daily program has little variance, routine being important to the stability of the child. The teacher should not vary either. I am confident the child will become calmer if he discovers a pattern in a person who has some degree of consistency.

After careful plans for routine, it is sometimes necessary for the teacher to alter the program to fit the situation. Nonessential restrictions should not be included, as the teacher can be more flexible if an infraction occurs. For major infractions of standards, there should be *no* flexibility. The reprimand should always be the same. In most cases of major infractions, the child is sent home for one or more days, not as punishment, but to make the child realize he is expected to follow instructions. After a few trips home, the child begins to realize school isn't so bad after all and will usually put forth an effort to follow standards.

Quiet periods or rest periods partially, if not totally, replace open recess time. This helps the NH child control himself and provides necessary rest for hyperactive children. Extended physical activity does not calm or quiet the NH youngster. He becomes more irritable and extremely difficult to work with.

The teacher must be very stable if he is to provide a mooring post for the NH child's frustration. Not enough can be said regarding the importance of the relationship between the NH child and his teacher. The teacher of the NH class is not only a teacher, but must also be a father, mother, nurse, baby sitter, playmate, and many other things to the NH child. He must make the child realize that he is really *for* him! There are many ways in which this can be accomplished successfully.

When the child has been sent home because of a major infraction of class standards, the teacher should visit the child's home and discuss the situation with the child and his parents. This should be done very calmly, letting the child and his parents know that the teacher is not alarmed and that he wants to help the child and is really "on his side." This is sometimes difficult to do. A friendly discussion in the child's home is more conducive to attaining this feeling than having a conference with the parents at school.

The same procedure could be followed when the child has had an exceptionally good day. If a home visit can't be arranged, a note or phone call should be arranged. If a note is sent home, the child should have the note read to him, or it might not reach home! It is a proud youngster, especially an NH youngster ,who can go home with a note of praise for a job well done.

Much progress can be made with the NH child's academic growth if the teacher and parents work together in establishing routines for the child in the home. This can be accomplished by holding monthly meetings with parents so that they may share each other's problems and successes and learn home techniques which have proved successful with other NH children. In some cases, it's necessary for the teacher to work with parents individually in setting home routines, with the teacher and parents sharing their knowledge of the child and constructing methods which can be most successful for him as an individual.

This then is "helping the child around the clock," but in my experience it is certainly worth the extra effort. It results in progress for the NH child, and in a growth of understanding for his parents, his teacher, and the school.

SECTION B

IDENTIFICATION

Chapter 3

DIAGNOSIS OF LEARNING DISABILITIES—
THE TEAM APPROACH

BERNICE V. GUNDERSON

T HE CHILD with learning disabilities has come to be a concern not only to educators but to those in other professions as well. If the educators are to give more than lip service to the slogan, "teach the whole child," areas other than the educational must also be considered in making a diagnosis.

There are indications that preliminary screening and identification can be done by school personnel, with additional consultants involved as indicated by the preliminary screening. In this team approach the key to success is communication and understanding. Progress has been made, defensiveness is gradually disappearing, and solutions are being sought. To begin, the pediatrician, perhaps more often than any other person, is sought out by parents of these children. As a result of his examination, he, in turn, may seek the help of the ophthalmologist, the neurologist, the orthopedist, the psychologist, the social worker, consultants at a mental health center, and other specialists. Only by viewing the total picture is it possible to help the child to maximum success in overcoming his problems and achieving in school.

For the purposes of assessing the total functional level of a child, the two major areas for concern are the (1) physical-environmental, and (2) the academic. By working within these two subdivisions answers to the following vital questions can be supplied: (1) What does the child bring to the educational

Reprinted from the *Journal Of Learning Disabilities*, Vol. 4 (1971), pp. 107-113. By permission of the author and publisher.

scene? (2) What has happened and is happening educationally?

Perhaps the most neglected area in the panorama of learning disabilities is the first question: What does this child bring to the educational scene?

I shall attempt to present an inventory of areas to assess, and to mention instruments or techniques which provide an *overall* profile of the child's strengths and weaknesses. On the basis of this profile, an academic program can be planned appropriate to the child's abilities thus making academic progress possible.

PEDIATRIC EXAMINATION

There are three general categories in the physical-environmental areas: (1) general physical condition, (2) environmental background, and (3) psychological-intellectual level of functioning. The area of general physical condition has been the one through which the pediatrician has entered the educational scene. A parent approaches the doctor (who most often has been caring for the child over a number of years) perhaps even before he approaches the school in regard to the problem or problems. The pediatrician examines the child and prepares a pediatric report, usually in narrative form, following this outline:

I. Family Background (interview)
   A. Parent-family review
      1. Age and health of parents
      2. Intellectual assessment of parents
      3. Stability of family
      4. Socioeconomic level
      5. Siblings and sibling history
      6. Patient's position within family (age, sibling relationships, parent-child relationships)
   B. Previous attempts at diagnosis
   C. Parent's statement of problem
II. Physical Examination
   A. Prenatal and neonatal history
      1. Gestational age
      2. Conditions of birth and postnatal period

        3. Early history (sat, walked, talked, activity level)

        4. Exceptional incidents (illnesses, accidents)

    B. Present physical condition

        1. Observations (office behavior)

        2. Results of physical examination (i.e. height, weight, vision, auditory, blood, noted abnormalities, neurological, speech, coordination.)

III. Educational Information

    A. Draw-a-person

    B. Alphabet and letters

    C. Reversals

    D. Vocabulary

    E. IQ (classification)

    F. School history, past and present

IV. Recommendations

    A. Definition of problem

    B. Medication, treatment, or further diagnosis recommended

        1. Home

        2. School

Within this framework are identified such things as parental expectations, intellectual level of the parents, birth injury, illnesses and accidents, behavioral problems, present health, together with a rather general assessment of intellectual and educational levels. If further diagnostic examination is indicated, the child is referred to the proper specialist. Perhaps an electroencephalogram, an ophthalmological or audiometric examination, routine laboratory tests, protein bound iodine, skull x-rays, genetic studies, or one of any number of types of examinations may be recommended. When these are completed, treatment and/or medication is prescribed.

For some of these children the diagnosis may include the words "minimal brain damage," or "hyperkinetic behavior syndrome." The report on these children may include descriptive comments such as "restless," "easily distracted," "short attention span," "unpredictable," or "hyperactive." The recommendations may include a prescription for one of several drugs used to help control the activity level of this type of child. These children must, of course, remain under the care and supervision of the doctor. The child's response to the medication cannot be measured by a scale or yardstick or a grade, but is dependent upon the opinion of those in close daily contact with him. Herein lies a great problem in regard to prescribing a drug, since the response to a medication varies with the individual and a trial and error process is necessary. The parent, too often resistant to the idea of drugs and/or the cost of the medication, is much too quick to say, "It hasn't helped at all." The teacher, desperate in attempting to control this restless distractable little person, is quick to respond favorably and perhaps to believe there has been greater benefit from the medication than there actually was. A trial of several weeks is necessary, as is an objective look at overall behavior improvement.

Drugs prescribed generally fall into three categories: (1) anticonvulsants, (2) stimulants, and (3) tranquilizers. The anticonvulsant, used to prevent or control seizure disorders, may be Dilantin® or one of several others. Stimulant-type drugs, such as Dexedrine® or Ritalin®, tend to slow down the hyperactive child and thus make living with him easier. Of the drugs available perhaps the one most often recommended is Dexedrine, which is reasonably inexpensive. If it proves ineffective, perhaps Ritalin, a more expensive drug, is tried. Mellaril® is recommended when aggressive and destructive manifestations of behavior are noted. Thorazine® has been effective for hyperactive, mentally retarded children. Valium® has been successful with one 15-year-old, emotionally disturbed boy in my experience. Checking and rechecking with the pediatrician is necessary in order to determine the correct dosage for the particular child.

It must be remembered that hyperactivity seldom appears alone as the only cause of the child's problems. Just as no man is an island, no facet of a child's life operates in isolation from the other facets which determine and direct his actions and reactions. The attitude and reaction to him of the others in his environment are a very important factor. Without doubt, the particular child under observation *does* function at a higher rate of speed than the average child. However, it is my opinion that all too often the reaction of parents contributes to the behavior pattern, and, indeed, tends to perpetuate it. Their reaction may take the way of overprotection; they may tend to become permissive and overlook undesirable behaviors, excusing him because he is "brain-damaged" or "hyperactive." Thus, they eliminate the very thing the child needs, i.e. structure and security in his environment. Other parents, themselves hypertense and hyperreactive, resort to screams, threats, and punishment, and a "snowballing" effect may be in operaton. The child, seeing that he gains attention in this way, responds with more of the same, and so on. A more positive approach is the use of encouragement and structured but kindly management, but this is difficult to maintain over a period of time.

Medication alone is not the total solution. Changes must be effected in the behaviors, reactions, and attitudes of both home and school. Nothing operates in isolaton. In this hyperactivity behavior syndrome, or minimal brain damage, several aspects must be considered: (1) Is the child *really* hyperactive, or is he merely more active than the average? (2) Is it possible that a maturational lag is causing the child to be less controllable than others his age? (3) Are family environmental conditions contributing to the behavior? (4) Is this child more emotionally disturbed than he is truly hyperactive? In any event, experience has shown that many of the manifestations of the hyperkinetic syndrome tend to diminish and by the end of adolescence have disappeared in most cases.

PSYCHOLOGICAL EXAMINATION

Apart from medical anomalies, a psychological assessment is another important area of concern. The major goal of the psychological evaluation is to determine some of the probable factors which may be contributing to the child's problems. The two main areas with which the psychologist concerns himself are intelligence and personality. By the administration of an intelligence test, the psychologist obtains an indicated level of ability. If the IQ is low or borderline, the child may well be functioning up to his ability level. Conversely, if the IQ score is average or above, then one can assume that other problems are interfering with the learning process. These may be emotional, neurological, physical, or cultural problems.

The two instruments most commonly in use for intellectual assessment are the Stanford-Binet test and the Wechsler Intelligence Scale for Children. One advantage of the WISC is that separate scores for verbal, performance, and full scale IQ are obtained, thus providing considerable information about the child. If this testing reveals a need, additional personality tests may be given.

It is not the purpose of this writing to elaborate on the merits or demerits of psychological test instruments or psychological testing per se. It is necessary to have an assessment of the indicated level of functioning. In interpretation of the scores and in drawing inferences from them are several things to bear in mind: (1) The test instruments most commonly used at the present time do, in part, reflect a measure of school learning and prior experience and not general intellectual potential alone. (2) Emotional reactions and a poor self-concept enter in to a greater degree than is usually taken into account. (3) Behavioral and attitudinal response patterns, learned and acquired, at times tend to prohibit the attaining of a truly accurate measure of innate potential, especially where children with learning disabilities are concerned. Too many other variables affect the results. The infallibility and long-term reliability of these test results on learning disabled children is being scrutinized and even questioned inasmuch as so many things affect their total score. However, a measure showing present indicated level of functioning is necessary, and testing by a certified school psychologist is therefore a necessary and revealing part of the overall picture.

SOCIAL WORKER'S ASSESSMENT OF HOME

This physical being, the learning disabled child, diagnostically examined by the pediatrician and intellectually evaluated by the psychologist, is not functioning in a vacuum, but in a home environment, the effects of which have been too greatly ignored and underrated. It is in the family unit where the child spends the greater portion of his time. In the final analysis, it is the family who is the most concerned about the child and his well-being, both physically and educationally. It is, then, only logical to look to the family of the child having problems. Herein the answers to many questions are found: (1) What degree of family stability is there? (2) Where within the family does this child fit? (3) What is the nature of the family relationships? (4) What is the socioeconomic level of the family? (5) What is the educational history of the family (parents and siblings)? (6) What standards and expectations does this family have? (7) What is the intellectual background of the family? (8) What has been the history of home-school relationships? (9) What is the parent's statement of the problem? By seeking and obtaining answers to the above questions vital clues to the "learning mystery" (or misery) are discovered. After one identifies the contributing factors, the way is open for discussion of ways to minimize any deleterious effects of the home environment. It is expected that the role of the school social worker will become increasingly important, since parents appear to be receptive to this interested, though apparently neutral, individual.

PARENT-TEACHER COMMUNICATION

The role of the social worker does not detract from the necessity of maintaining open lines of communication between home and school. Parent-teacher communication is a must if the ultimate in academic success is going to be possible for the child. It has been my experience that asking the parent (or parents) what the child's problem is reveals their level of awareness and thus points the way for further explanation and/or conversation regarding the difficulties the child is encountering at school. There are several "conference commandments" which are conducive to a greater measure of success with parents: (1) Pose the question, "What do you see as the child's problem?" (2) Be honest; do not "skirt" the problem or problems. (3) Include positives as well as negatives in order to make the parents better able to accept what is said. (4) Adjust your vocabulary level to that of the parents. If they do not understand what you are saying, then you are not communicating. (5) Be a good listener; let the parent supply you with information. Often, the answers to many questions to which the school seeks answers may be found here.

EDUCATIONAL EVALUATION

The final area to survey in regard to the learning disabled child is the educational arena. Perhaps it is here that, for the first time, the child encounters noticeable difficulties.

Preliminary screening can well be done through observation by the classroom teacher. A teacher check list with the following items provides a preview, so to speak, of the educational picture the child presents.

I. Physical

Is clean and well-cared for
Often appears tired
Comes without breakfast
Is frequently absent
Appears average in size (for age, etc.)
Is overweight
Appears undernourished
Poorly coordinated
Appears to have visual problems
Appears to have auditory problems
Has other physical impairments
Specify:
Has speech and language problems
Teeth need care
Body dominance problems
Immature habits (thumb sucking, nail biting)
Appears mentally retarded

II. Behavioral—Attitudinal

Applies himself to best of ability
Fails to complete work
Wastes time
Annoys others
Daydreams
Always out of his seat
Easily distracted
Short attention span

Demands much attention
Relates to peers poorly
Relates to teacher poorly
Is often cruel
Hyperactive and restless
Is undependable
Is well behaved
Is upset easily
Is destructive and/or explosive
Is stubborn and uncooperative
Seems sad and unhappy
Has poor self-concept
Has emotional problems
Enjoys school
Dislikes school
Is happy and well adjusted

III. Educational

Has repeated a grade
Continues to have reversal problems
Confuses letters
Lacks knowledge of letter names
Lacks interest and motivation
Has trouble following directions
Receives speech therapy
Receives individual tutoring
Meager vocabulary knowledge
Lacks knowledge of specific word meanings
Is below grade level in reading
Is below grade level in math
Is below grade level in spelling
Dislikes reading
Dislikes math
Lacks skill in basic phonics and word analysis
Makes many reading errors
Has poor comprehension
Poor at blending word sounds
Moves head as he reads
Moves lips as he reads silently
Has other abilities (art, music, etc.)
Is a problem student, generally
Has auditory problems in academic areas
Has visual problems in academic areas
Poor home cooperation overall
Good home cooperation overall

From this, further steps can be taken to reveal the details of the picture and to determine what diagnostic measures are indicated.

The educational consultant (or reading specialist) will also be interested in the previous academic history of the child, including such things as the child's present age and grade level, grades repeated, onset of the problem, previous attempts at diagnosis, previous attempts at remediation, teacher's statement of problem, and so forth. Some insight into the difficulty may be gained by asking the child what his problems are. It has come to my attention that many learning disabled children are convinced that they are mentally retarded, even though their IQ may actually be well above that level.

In addition to using observation and interviews, there are some informal ways of testing the child on some of the checklist items. The following are some specific areas to check:

1. Speech and language. Have him repeat words and sentences. Notice his articulation.

2. Gross motor. Can he skip, hop, and so forth? How does he walk?

3. Spatial-orientation, body balance, and the like. Check him on a balance beam. Have him lie on the floor and give him directions such as: touch your right hand to your left ear; place

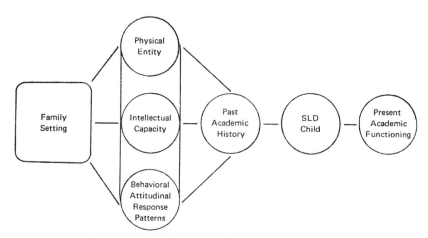

Figure 3-1. The SLD Child—An Overview.

your left hand to your left ear; place your left hand on your left knee; and so forth.

4. Body-dominance. Have him throw a ball, kick a football, sight through a paper tube, and so on.

5. Names of the letters of the alphabet. Does he know the letter names?

6. Beginning sounds. Can he recognize words which begin with the same sound?

7. Counting and numbers. How far can he count? Is he able to recognize and read numbers?

8. Writing and fine-motor. Can he write his name? Dictate numbers, letters, and words, and watch for reversal tendencies.

9. Auditory discrimination. Stand behind the child and check his hearing accuracy on initial sounds, final sounds, and medial sounds. Pronounce two words, and have the child respond "same" or "not the same." The following may be used: map, map; can, tan; map, nap; rap, rap; bun, but; rip, rib; ring, rink; road, rolled; thing, think; rust, rush; much, must; bed, big.

10. Auditory memory. Repeat numbers, letters, and words in a series, and ask him to say them back to you; seven, six; six, nine, two; four, three, two, seven; n b s; r t g; a b t o; come, see, go; nine, three, one; man, table, book, star; do, see, think, run, go.

If difficulties are detected in this informal testing remedial effort can be directed to those areas.

There remains then the formal educational evaluation of the child. While the test instruments are an important source of specific information about the child, much additional and vital information can be obtained by careful observation of the child as he is being tested. Things to note include (1) general physical condition and appearance, (2) emotional reactions, (3) distractibility, (4) nervousness, (5) restlessness and inattentiveness, (6) method of operation or attack, (7) general attitude, and (8) noticeable visual or auditory problems.

It seems essential to any evaluation of a child's level of academic functioning to include some measure for assessing his level of intellectual ability. If psychological examination is not a part of the total evaluation, the classroom teacher should utilize an intelligence test of some sort (such as Peabody Picture Vocabulary Test, or the Otis Lennon). If the child is having difficulty in learning, the first area to scrutinize is his intellectual ability. In a sense, the question is, Does he have it or doesn't he?

The area of reading, where the child's problems are often first noted, has several operational skills that can be assessed: (1) vocabulary level, (2) reading level, (3) comprehension, (4) phonics, and (5) word analysis. Initially the use of the Botel Word Recognition Test or the Dolch Word List provides a quick way of obtaining an approximate reading level. This tells the examiner the approximate level at which to attempt to obtain an oral and/or silent reading test score. Any of the presently available standardized reading tests, such as the Durrell Analysis of Reading Difficulty, or the Spache Diagnostic Reading Scales, will provide this as well as the child's level of comprehension. The child's knowledge in the area of phonics can be surveyed through use of the Botel Phonics Test or the phonics section from a diagnostic reading test. Included in the total test battery should be a measure of visual-motor ability (such as the Beery-Buktenica Developmental Test of Visual-Motor Integration), a test on visual-memory (the Durrell Analysis of Reading Difficulty has a good one), and a test of visual-perception (such as The Southern California Figure-Ground Visual Perception Test or the Science Research Associates Primary Mental Abilities Test). Mathematics, spelling, and motor proficiency should also be assessed. Many tests or portions of tests are available for these.

It is only by utilizing a team approach and surveying the child as a total entity, (see Fig. 3-1), that one can determine that the cause itself, and not just a symptom, is being treated.

REFERENCES

1. Ayres, A. Jean: *Southern California Figure-Ground Visual Perception Test.* Beverly Hills, Western Psychol. Services, 1966.
2. Beery, Keith E., and Buktenica, Norman: *Developmental Test of Visual-Motor Integration.* Chicago, Follett Educ., 1967.
3. Botel, Morton: *Botel Reading Inventory.* Chicago, Follett, 1966.
4. Dolch, E. W.: *Dolch Word Lists.* Illinois, Garrard, 1953.
5. Dunn, Lloyd M.: *Peabody Picture Vocabulary Test.* Minnesota, Guidance Service, 1959.

6. Durrell, Donald D.: *Durrell Analysis of Reading Difficulty.* New York, Harcourt, Brace & World, 1955.
7. Otis, Arthur, and Lennon, Roger: *Mental Ability Test.* New York, Harcourt, Brace & World, 1967.
8. Spache, George D.: *Diagnostic Reading Scales.* New York, McGraw-Hill, 1965.
9. Terman, L. M., and Merrill, Maud: *Stanford-Binet Intelligence Scales.* Massachusetts, Houghton, 1960.
10. Thurstone, L. L., and Thurston, Thelma G.: *Primary Mental Abilities.* Chicago, Sci. Res. Assoc., 1962.
11. Wechsler, David: *Wechsler Intelligence Scale for Children.* New York, Psychological Corp., 1955.

Chapter 4

THREE APPROACHES TO DIAGNOSIS AND EDUCATIONAL PLANNING FOR CHILDREN WITH LEARNING DISABILITIES

BARBARA BATEMAN

A FIELD which has experienced the phenomenal upsurge in growth and interest that has characterized learning disabilities in recent years is bound to be beset by diverse terminology, procedures, and views. To so describe learning disabilities today is quite probably an understatement. The marriage for which Clements pleads between what he considers only two differing views within the field might be thoroughly polygamous, should it occur.[4]

While there is little substantial agreement on definition, incidence, or remedial procedures, there is almost universal agreement on the need for diagnosis of children with learning problems. But agreement on the need for diagnosis does not produce conformity in the diagnostic procedures used. There has been striking divergence among the diagnostic philosophies and techniques seen in recent years.

ETIOLOGICAL APPROACH

This paper describes three approaches to the educational diagnosis of children with learning problems. These approaches are neither mutually exclusive nor irreconcilable. Some diagnosticians use all three. The first might be called the etiological approach. The ultimate hope of the field with respect to prevention and scientific treatment probably lies in more definitive knowledge of the causes of learning problems. Such knowledge

Reprinted from the *Academic Therapy Quarterly*, Vol. 2 (1967), pp. 215-222. By permission of the author and publisher.

of etiological factors may also eventually provide the best basis of grouping for educational planning. Alex Bannatyne's classification of types of dyslexia with respective remedial techniques is a step in this direction.[1] We need even more extensive data on the validity and efficacy of relating subtle etiological factors in learning disorders to differential remedial programs. Some of the problems of investigating relationships between etiology and remediation include the multiple and interacting causative factors in which may operate in a given case the lack of one-to-one correspondence between etiology and observed behavior (perhaps due to our imprecision in assessing both), and the lack of clear differentiation among remedial techniques on the basis of the principles of learning or teaching on which they are based.

At this stage of our knowledge, the pursuit of etiological factors as a sole approach to educational planning sometimes proves frustrating. Among the several disciplines directly concerned and involved with children with learning problems, educators often receive the most direct pressure to devise and execute a plan of action for remediating the child's difficulties. Specifically, their concern is with what and how to teach a child who has already demonstrated that he learns differently and not very readily those things the educator is charged with teaching him. The disciplines primarily concerned with etiology are sometimes one or more steps removed from this necessity of everyday, hour-by-hour contact with the child in a formal learning situation. Among the major diagnostic interests of those concerned with etiology are the past factors which contributed to the present status (case history) and accurate comparison of symptoms with known diagnostic categories or syndromes (classification). But these kinds of data, valuable as they are in their own right, do not always serve the additional purpose, so necessary to educators, of providing clear-cut direction as to how and what to teach the child. In the early 1960's, special education literature reflected concern over this gap between etiologically oriented diagnosis and remedial planning.[10] This was occasionally seen when remedially oriented teachers and etiologically oriented psychologists experienced difficulty in communicating with each other.

DIAGNOSTIC-REMEDIAL APPROACH

The need for bridging the gap between etiologically oriented diagnosis and remedial planning gave impetus to a second approach which might be called the diagnostic-remedial approach. Assessment instruments such as the Illinois Test of Psycholinguistic Abilities (ITPA), the Frostig Developmental Tests of Visual Perception, and the Purdue Perceptual Rating Scale were prime movers in this approach. One of the core ideas in this approach is that of "correlated disabilities." The diagnostic-remedial approach de-emphasizes the concept of causation and concentrates on basic disabilities in perceptual, integrative, or expressive functions which are reflected in the presenting academic or behavioral inadequacy. For example, a child who has been unable to learn to read might be found to score very poorly on measures of auditory closure of visual memory. The auditory closure or visual memory deficit would then be seen as a correlated disability, and initial remedial efforts would be directed toward that disability. The distinction between a correlated disability and a causal factor is at the same time artificial and real. It is artificial in that one could argue that within this framework the diagnostician is really postulating that the auditory closure deficit caused the reading disability and that is the very reason he plans remediation for the closure problem. But the distinction is also real in that the tracing of causal factors stops there, rather than continuing, as it would in the etiological approach, to probe why the closure problem exists, or what caused it. The etiologically oriented diagnostician might find, through further testing or case history data, that the auditory closure problem was caused by temporal lobe damage. But temporal lobe damage does not tell the teacher what to teach and might even have the unfortunate result of making her feel that teaching was futile; an auditory closure problem tells her to teach sound blending. The distinction between a correlated disability and an etiological factor thus becomes real in practice. It also becomes clear that some educators' objections to the etiologic approach are to the diagnostician's method of reporting his findings rather than to the kind of procedures he used. This problem has been seen in the field in the many discussions, articles, and meetings on the topic of how school psychologists could make their reports more meaningful to teachers.

The diagnostic-remedial process frequently is addressed to the question of how to teach, as well as what to teach, as discussed above. Once the child's pattern of perceptual, integrative, and expressive strengths and weakness has been reliably assessed and verified, a decision must be made as to whether he should be taught by methods which capitalize on his strengths or require exercise of his weaknesses. Both strategies have been recommended by authorities. Cohn advocates uitlizing the intact or strong modality for presentation of material[5]; while S. A. Kirk recommends teaching to the weakness.[9] Thus, it is theoretically possible that the same diagnostic test data given to various learning disability specialists would lead to different remedial recommendations.

Most persons in the field seem to implicitly agree that there is an interaction between subject and method, and that one does somehow derive individualized remedial approaches from this child-study approach. However, data to support this implicit subject-method interaction assumption needs to be made known. At least two studies falied to obtain the expected interaction.[2, 8]

Another problem sometimes encountered within the diagnostic-remedial approach is that of the relationship between improvement in the correlated disability and improvement in the presenting academic difficulty. For example, more research on the effectiveness of visual perception training in increasing reading ability is believed by some to be necessary. Even in those cases where remediation directed to the correlated disability has clearly led to later improvement in the academic area, the question can be raised as to whether remediating the academic problem directly might not have been just as effective and possibly more efficient. The plea for more research is made almost apologetically these days, yet the need is strikingly obvious in regard to these kinds of questions.

A last question which has been raised concerning the diagnostic-remedial approach to learning disabilities is that of how much direction it actually does provide in planning remedial activities. This problem has been cogently and incisively ex-

plored by S. Engelmann in an article which might well be
required reading for all persons interested in testing or teaching
children.[6] Engelmann's case against the utility of the concepts
of correlated disabilities, perceptual disabilities, on psycholinguistic disabilities, as aids to educational planning is so tightly
reasoned and sequenced it is difficult to summarize adequately.
One of his major points, however, is that the usual recommendations which result from the approach are too inclusive; e.g. teach
auditory discrimination, associations, vocal encoding, figure-
ground discrimination, or proved sensory stimulation. Engelmann points out:

> The usual assertion is that the "directions" offered by such instru-
> ments as the Illinois Test of Psycholinguistic Abilities are of some
> value, because, although test results do not imply specific tasks, they
> imply general educational directions—but the allegation that general
> direction is better than no direction at all is not as attractive as it
> may seem upon casual inspection. The flaw in this argument is that
> the teacher is not without direction in the first place. (p. 94)

According to Englemann, if the diagnostic instruments from
which the diagnosis was made contain educationally relevant
items which are failed by the child, then he should be taught
those items; if they contain educationally irrelevant items, they
further cloud the question of what to teach. He objects that
inclusive remedies, such as "teach vocal encoding" or "teach
visual memory," generate both relevant and irrelevant tasks and
the burden of selection remains, as it originally was, on the
teacher; thus, the diagnosis has been of no help.

Mann and Phillips[11] have also criticized the diagnostic-
remedial approach, which they call "fractional." The ITPA and
Frostig tests and remedial implications come under close and
critical scrutiny. Their criticisms of the fractionators include

> . . . their often facile extrapolation of unsettled and controversial
> experimental and theoretical issues into educational and clinical
> dicta and practice; their establishment of techniques of uncertain
> and, at best, limited validity as prime diagnostic and treatment
> instruments; their seeming disregard of the handicapped child as a
> unitary, though complex, organism; their approach to him as a col-
> lection of discrete and isolated functions. (p. 311)

They also point out the problem of validity of claims for "therapeutic efficacy of fractional instruments. The most immediate and glaring error is seen in attempts to demonstrate their value through tests that have a close facsimilitude to the training devices themselves."[11, p. 315] We will all welcome the end of the studies whch attempt, for example, to demonstrate the efficacy of psycholingustic training through increased scores on the ITPA and the vice versa. But in fairness to the developers of the ITPA it should be recalled that in the early stages of this instrument a crucial question was whether or not the functions measured were subject to change through remediation. The acceptance of the concepts of educability of cognitive abilities is now so widespread that we tend to forget that a few years ago there was a real need to demonstrate that psycholinguistic abilities could be improved before getting on to the more important business of refining the remedial techniques. But the prolongation of this early type of research is regrettable and hopefully in the near future the efficacy of remediation will be judged by improvement in areas such as reading, writing, and speaking.

TASK-ANALYSIS APPROACH

A third approach to diagnosing learning problems might be described as the task-analysis approach. This is very similar to what Engelmann has called the educational deficit approach (in contrast to the diagnostic-remedial or personal inadequacy approach) to educational planning.[6] It relies heavily on concepts from the behaviorist view of how to modify performance. In a review of two recent volumes on learning disorders, T. M. Stephens[12] noted:

> Considerable space is devoted to an interesting attempt to relate psychological and neurological diagnostic information about one child to academic instruction. The discerning reader will note that the teacher's approach . . . had little relevance to the great amount of diagnostic data. In fact, both volumes fail to show how to bridge the gap between diagnosis and instruction. And, amazingly, the emerging body of knowledge that clearly bridges this chasm, the various forms of behavioristic psychology, is not presented in either volume. (p. 164)

In this behavioristic task-analysis approach there is a relative deemphasis on assumed processes within the child and more emphasis on what specific educational tasks he needs to be taught. A related emphasis is placed on analyzing the tasks to be taught into their component sequential steps.

A discussion of behaviorist psychology is beyond the immediate focus of this paper, but clearly some behavior modification techniques and principles are now being applied in this task-analysis approach to diagnosing and remediating children's learning problems.[13] The approach is characterized by the question, What specific behavior does the child need to be taught? The answer is sought by observation of performance on educationally relevant tasks, such as attending school, counting, use of prepositions, sitting still, completing assignment, and attending to the teacher when she is the relevant stimulus. The test instruments beginning to appear are criterion-referenced rather than norm-referenced. Even though the task analysis approach per se is just beginning to be discussed in learning-ability circles, it is already meeting all the expected objections raised in the past about behavior modification, i.e. it is too cold and mechanistic, not enough attention is paid to the whole child. In addition, there is another question somewhat more demanding of serious reply, namely, How do you select the tasks to be taught? Here, the problems of educational philosophy, the role of the school, and the primary responsibility of the teacher rise up in full force. Every one of us might use slightly different selection criteria, depending on our personal value system, our beliefs concerning the proper role of education in our society, and our knowledge of what skills are truly prerequisite to which outcomes.

One view of task selection or curriculum development which has elements of both the diagnostic-remedial and the task-analysis approaches is that of R. Valett, who proposes a classification and arrangement of basic developmental tasks for teacher use.[14] He has selected 229 test items (some from tests such as the Binet and WISC), which presumably have educational relevance, and has arranged them in a development sequence under the headings: Motor Integration and Physical Development, Tactile Discrimination, Auditory Discrimination, Language Development and Verbal Fluency, Visual-Motor Coordination, and Conceptual Development. Those items failed by the child are scrutinized, and areas of specific, individualized training needs are developed. While the headings under which the items are grouped and the name of the instrument itself, The Valett Developmental Survey of Basic Learning Abilities, suggest something of the concept of the diagnostic-remedial approach, the specific attention to educational tasks and the direct teaching of test items are both characteristic of the task-analysis approach.

A curriculum-building effort which belongs solely to the task-analysis approach is that of Berister and Engelmann.[13] While Valett asks the norm-referenced question, "When do other children ordinarily learn certain tasks?" Berister and Engelmann ask the criterion-referenced question, "What does this child need to be taught in order to accomplish a specified educational outcome?" Given the outcome of being able to succeed in a first-grade school experience, they postulated fifteen specific tasks to be taught to the preschooler, and these fifteen tasks became the core of the preschool curriculum. They devised highly specific teaching techniques (e.g. a uniquely clean teaching presentation for color concepts) and more general teaching strategies (e.g. unison responses rather than individual responses.) The problem of differential learning rates has by no means been solved in this curriculum, nor has the problem of what to do when a child doesn't learn, even with the clean teaching method. However, one of the many significant emphases of their volume is that a teacher's basic premise is set forth: If the child hasn't yet learned, he hasn't yet successfully been taught.

The following story is probably more myth than truth, but is worth repeating. When a college class of education majors were taking experimental psychology, they were each required to teach a certain maze-running pattern to a rat. Some of the students' rats did not learn the maze as rapidly as other students' rats. But not one of the future teachers whose rat had failed to learn assumed their rat was brain-injured or even deficient in maze-running ability. Rather, they all assumed that something had been wrong with their teaching technique. This is one of the messages from task-analysis to learning disabilities, and perhaps from science to education.

Another message from task-analysis is that goals absolutely

must be clearly defined before appropriate teaching strategies can be devised. "Put a man on the moon by 1970" is a highly specific goal which has proven capable of generating a great deal of activity. Whether or not one agrees with the appropriateness or value of the goal, it is still eminently possible to map out procedures for its implementation. In teaching children, we need to have highly specific goals, and task-analysis facilitates this process of goal establishment, even though it may not solve all the implementation problems. While it is quite conceivable that even in the best of all educational worlds there would still be some children with learning problems, it is just as conceivable that judicious application of the task-analysis approach would leave us with a somewhat smaller group of these children than we currently have.

SUMMARY

Earlier it was said that all three approaches—etiological, diagnostic-remedial, and task-analysis—can be utilized by one diagnostician. At this point it might be urged that all three should be used, as each has a potential contribution to make to our knowledge about learning problems, even though they might not contribute equally to educational planning per se. The summary chart below illustrates in a deliberately exaggerated fashion the type of comments which might appear in the final lines of a diagnostic report written within the confines of each of the three approaches described in this paper. All have a place, all have similarities, and all have a unique emphasis. The accomplished diagnostician is able to utilize the contributions and avoid the pitfalls of all.

REFERENCES

1. Bannatyne, Alex: Diagnostic and remedial techniques for use with dyslexic children. *Word Blind Bulletin*, 1:4-15, Winter, 1966.
2. Bateman, Barbara: Reading; a controversial view—research and rationale. *Curriculum Bulletin*, 23:278, May 1967.
3. Berister, C., and Engelmann, S.: *Teaching Disadvantaged Children in the Preschool.* Engelwood Cliffs, Prentice-Hall, 1966.
4. Clements, Sam D.: Come to the wedding. *Academic Therapy Quarterly*, 2:134-138, Spring 1967.

SUMMARY CHART

	Etiological	Diagnostic-Remedial	Task-Analysis
Case 1	Primary language disorder of an expressive aphasoid type due to organic impairment resulting from anoxia. Recommend special education placement.	Deficiencies in vocal encoding, auditory-vocal automatic, and auditory-vocal association. Slight weakness in auditory decoding. Teach language structures, reasoning, and general conversational speech.	Does not use, and therefore should be taught, the following language statement patterns: This is a ——. This is not a ——. This is a ——. This is not big, it is ——. Does not form plurals of nouns, or use past tenses of verbs. Uses "and" for both "or" and "and," etc.
Case 2	Mentally retarded, familial origin. Eligible for EMH class. Binet I.Q. 67.	Shows typical psycholinguistic profile for retarded youngster. Visual-motor functioning two years above auditory-vocal, with particular deficiencies in rote and segmental abilities. Needs drill and memory training.	Does not name body parts; does not generate descriptive statements, such as this is a girl reading a book; does not know basic colors.
Case 3	Minimal brain dysfunction, average intellectual potential. Eligible for placement in special learning disability class.	Motor encoding and visual decoding disability characteristic of Strauss Syndrome. Short attention span and moderate hyperactivity. Recommend a highly structured classroom and special attention to sensory-motor training.	Needs to be taught to sit at desk for increasing periods of time. Teach letter formation with increasing demands for precision. Balance could be improved by walking-board exercises.

REPRESENTATIVE DATA SOURCES

Etiological	Diagnostic-Remedial	Task-Analysis
Case history Medical and neurological exams EEG Psychometric tests such as WISC	Illinois Test of Psycholinguistic Ability Frostig Test of Visual Perception Wepman's Test of Auditory Discrimination Purdue Perceptual Motor Survey	Reading tests Baseline observations Basic concept inventory[7] Achievement tests

5. Cohn, R.: The neurological study of children with learning disabilities. *Exceptional Child, 31*:179-185, December 1964.
6. Engelmann, S.: Relationship between psychological theories and the act of teaching. *J School Psychol, 2*:93-100 Winter 1967.
7. ———*Basic Concept Inventory.* Chicago, Follett, In press.
8. Harris, A. J.: *Individualizing First-Grade Reading According to Specific Learning Aptitudes.* City University of New York, Office of Research and Evaluation, Division of Teacher Education, April 1965. (Mimeographed.)
9. Kirk, S. A.: *Educating Exceptional Children.* Boston, Houghton Mifflin, 1962.
10. ——— and McCarthy, J. J.: The ITPA—An approach to differential diagnosis. *Am J Ment Defic, 66*:399-412, November 1961.
11. Mann, L., and Phillips, W. A.: Fractional practices in special education: A critique. *Excep Child, 33*:311-317, January 1967.
12. Stephens, T. M.: *Review of Learning Disorders,* 2 vols., Jerome Hellmuth, (Ed.) (Seattle, Special Child, 1965). *J School Psychol, 2*: 163-164, Winter 1967.
13. Ullman, L. P., and Krasner, L.: *Case Studies in Behavior Modification.* New York, Holt, Rinehart and Winston, 1965.
14. Valett, R.: A developmental task approach to early childhood education. *J School Psychol, 2*:136-147, Winter 1967.

Chapter 5

DIAGNOSING LEARNING DISABILITIES AND WRITING REMEDIAL PRESCRIPTIONS

ALEX BANNATYNE

Diagnosis is a concept with many labels, and many people in different disciplines or having different viewpoints may choose a particular term to their liking. Some part-synonyms used for discovering what is wrong with fellow human beings are assesment, evaluation, task-analysis, investigation, checkup, finding out, observing behavior, and problem-solving. We will not be far away from a satisfactory definition of diagnosis if we accept Webster's three versions and slightly modify them. On this basis, a diagnosis is the act or process of deciding the nature of a disorder or disability by examination and through the examination making a careful investigation of the facts to determine the nature or basis of the problem. The final diagnosis is the decision from such an examination or investigation.

It is a little less easy to give a satisfactory definition of learning disabilities. The essential aspect of a learning disability is a discrepancy between the child's apparent potential and his performance in practice when he has to carry out some essential learning process. The learning disability itself is not primarily caused by inadequate mental ability, emotional disturbance, or sensorimotor organ defects. Of course, it is quite possible for a child with learning disabilities to also have defective sensory apparatus (for example, defective vision), to be mentally retarded, or to exhibit some form of emotional instability.

The remediation of learning disabilities will almost always

Reprinted from the *Journal Of Learning Disabilities*, Vol. 1 (1968), pp. 242-249. By permission of the author and instructor.

require specialized teaching techniques. Learning disabilities usually manifest themselves in disturbances of global end-result complex behavior, such as reading, and like the proverbial iceberg, they are nine-tenths hidden. Just as there are hundreds of reasons why a person may not be able to walk, so are there hundreds of possible discrete causal states which can result in the inability to learn to calculate, read, write, or spell well. This is equally true for most other academic studies in which the child may engage. Not infrequently, several separate specific deficits may combine in a multifaceted disability to make the diagnosis and remediation quite complicated.

TEAM DIAGNOSIS

To ensure an unbiased, accurate diagnostic examination, a team of specialists should work together with the child. The key members of the team, some of whom may be part-time, are an educator, psychologist, speech correctionist, pediatrician, and social worker. It will be obvious from the account of the diagnostic procedure below which team member investigates and supplies specific data and information. Either the educator or the psychologist should be the executive director of the team, both of whom should have been trained in the field of learning disabilities. Other experts, such as an E.E.G. specialist, or psychiatrist, may be consulted as the team thinks necessary. In fact, an E.E.G., electropolymyographs, a physical checkup, and an audiometry test should be obligatory in all cases.

THE PURPOSE OF DIAGNOSIS

The diagnostic objective must be the remediation of the deficit areas and the guiding rule should be, "remediate the deficit areas and reinforce through the intact areas." For example, if a boy had an auditory discrimination problem, one would thoroughly train him in phoneme discrimination, and if his writing ability was intact, he would be asked to write down for record purposes the mistaken (and corrected) words in which the difficult phonemes were presented auditorially, thus reinforcing the corrected discriminations through motor-kinesthetic activity. The word reinforce is used here in its original meaning and not as an operant reward.

From what has been said, it will be apparent that it is essential not to miss any area or facet of the child which might be contributing to the end-result learning disability either on the surface or manifest level, or on any of the other supporting levels which are less obvious. I shall describe each of the four major levels which require diagnostic analysis, indicate the tests and information used on each level, and describe cross-analyzing the data for the isolation of deficits.

THE ACADEMIC LEVEL

This is the area in which most teachers and many psychologists usually investigate the child's problems. Almost any of the major better-known achievement tests are valuable as an overall screening of the academic attainment of individual children or groups. It is very important to note, not only the school subjects in which the child does well or poorly but also his areas of success and failure with each subject. Even on achievement tests, indicators can be found as to which sensorimotor or cognitive skills are tending to lower the child's performance. Two useful reading tests are to be found in the Gates-McKillop Reading Tests and the Neale Analysis of Reading Ability.[1] The Gates-McKillop is a very long test and the following sections may be left out if time is short: Words Flashed, Phrases Flashed, Recognition and Blending, Naming Capitals, Recognizing Nonsense Words, Recognizing Initial Letters, Recognizing Final Letters, and Vocabulary Syllabification. The Neale Reading Test has three scores: Accuracy, Comprehension, and Rate of Reading. The implications of each of these three scores in the final analysis of the data should be taken into account, although the comprehension score is (as are so many comprehension scores) mostly a test of verbal memory. The child should be examined for his knowledge of phoneme/grapheme matchings by using the flash cards in the *Writing Road to Reading* by Spalding and Spalding. Another academic test whch may be found useful is the Ayres Spelling Test. However, there is a great need for a standardized comprehensive spelling test which not only examines the child both orally and in writing but also on words with a regular orthography and separately on words with an irregular orthography. The child's handwriting can be assessed from his written spelling, but he should also be given the opportunity to write as well as he is able.

It should be noted that if learning disability children make an intensive effort, many can produce quite good work, possibly near the class average, but it should always be remembered that this requires a very special effort which is not demanded of most normal children on an everyday basis. Within all these tests on the academic level, one can make quite a detailed diagnosis of the specific points with which the child needs help. However, it is quite possible that intensive instruction only on the academic level may not result in the rapid progress expected simply because more fundamental deficits underlie the child's problems with his school work.

COGNITIVE AND SENSORIMOTOR ABILITY LEVEL

There are several major tests which should be given on this level and the Wechsler Intelligence Scale for Children is an essential one. The Stanford-Binet Intelligence Scale is far too verbal and unstructured in content and presentation for the assessment of learning disability cases. All of the subtests of the W.I.S.C. except Mazes should be administered and the child's full-scale, verbal, and performance I.Q.'s calculated. However, it is now well known from factor analytic studies that the verbal and performance breakdown scores do not have much psychological meaning, I have found it more useful to analyze the W.I.S.C. in the following way:[5]

A Spatial score is obtained by adding together the scaled scores of three of the performance subtests which do not involve sequencing. They are

Picture Completion + Block Design + Object Assembly.

The Conceptualizing score is compiled from scaled scores:

Comprehension + Similarities + Vocabulary

A Sequencing score is obtained by combining the scaled scores for

Digit Span + Picture Arrangement + Coding

The composite mean standardized scaled scores expected for each of these groupings of three subtests is thirty. By comparing a child's spatial score with his conceptualizing and sequencing score, one can obtain just that much more information as to where the child's deficit areas lie. Many Genetic Dyslexic children (Bannatyne[3]) will obtain a good spatial score and a poor sequencing score when these are compared with their overall ability, their deficit being more in auditory closure and sequencing.

The next major test in the cognitive and sensorimotor abilities level is the Illinois Test of Psycholinguistic Ability. A revised version, which is being published at the moment (Kirk,[4]) contains twelve subtests: Auditory Reception, Visual Reception, Visual Sequencing Memory, Visual Association, Visual Closure, Verbal Expression, Grammar Closure, Manual Expression, Auditory Closeup, and Sound Blending. A profile drawn in accordance with the instructions in the handbook will immediately indicate many of the child's deficits and strengths.

The third major test is the Frostig Development Test of Visual Perception.[5] The Frostig Test has five subtests: Eye-Motor Coordination, Figure-Ground, Form Constancy, Position in Space, and Spatial Relations. This test is valuable for a quite detailed analysis of a child's visuospatial ability and visual perception in two dimensions.

Other tests which should be given for a complete diagnosis are the Graham-Kendall Memory-for-Designs Test,[6] which investigates just that—the child's memory for designs. However, as we are not investigating brain damage per se, but rather the child's ability to learn particular subjects, I have found that four or more errors of any kind on the M-F-D indicate the likelihood of a visuospatial or visuomotor disability of some kind. Most children nine years old and over who have no problems in this area will correctly remember and draw all the designs except perhaps for one or two exact reversals. A useful back-up copying test in this area is the Beery-Buktenica Developmental Form Sequence Test.[7] Here again, the older child should be able to copy all of these designs reasonably well, always allowing, of course, for one or two unintentional mistakes. A repeat test is always advisable.

A useful auditory discrimination test is the Wepman[8] or one issued by the Perceptual and Educational Research Center.[9] Here again, most normal children should attain an almost perfect score. Charles Drake suggests that more than five errors are indicative of an auditory discrimination problem which may need even more investigation. As auditory discrimination tests are very unreliable, one should always tape them using a clear, woman's voice and administer them twice with a week's interval between tests. As a consequence of the findings of two research projects separately carried out by Drake and Schnall (1966) and Wolf[10] (1967), we know that one excellent diagnostic indicator of auditory reading disabilities is the Melody Discrimination Test. I have made up my own version using a xylophone. Ten pairs of four-note melodies, some pairs being the same and some different, were recorded on tape allowing five-second intervals for answering. If the diagnostician can play the piano, an informal test of this sort could be recorded and administered to each child.

The Money Road Map Test of Direction Sense[11] and the Benton Right/Left Discrimination Test[12] will assess the child's understanding of the concepts right and left and indicate the extent of any confusion. His handedness can be investigated using the Harris Laterality Scale.[13] The simultaneous writing subtest of this scale is a useful indicator of reversals by either hand but only if the child is asked to perform very quickly. Sometimes a nominally right-handed subject will reverse (mirror image) the right-hand letters but not the left ones, indicating he is basically left-handed. However, I never advise changing hands unless the change is quite spontaneous.

PERSONALITY, EMOTIONAL, MOTIVATIONAL, LEVEL

One of the most useful sources of information on this level is the Family Information Form which the parents have to fill in at home. The questions cover the following topics: (1) the number and order of siblings, (2) the walking, toilet training, and feeding milestones, (3) speech acquisition, (4) mother-child separation, (5) symptoms of neurosis or other emotional disturbance, (6) family language background and development, (7) the child's physical development, mostly in terms of clumsiness, (18) the incidence of learning disabilities in other members of the family, (9) the occupation of the father and mother, and (10) the number of schools and types of classes the child has been to. The mother is also asked for a full pregnancy, birth, and subsequent medical history of the child and, if possible, this should be cross-checked with medical informants.

A psychologist should be asked for a personality assessment of the child (I have found the Bene-Anthony Family Relations[14] to be of value in assessing the child's attitudes to the members of his family. Some assessment of the amount of anxiety exhibited by the child is also useful). The Sarason Test Anxiety Scale and General Anxiety Scale[15] can be used for this purpose. Other orthodox projective techniques can be administered by experienced clinical psychologists.

A careful winnowing out of the child's genuine interests in life will help in the remedial planning of high interest work programs and literature selection. A lengthy check-list combined with a conversational approach should prove effective here.

NEUROPHYSIOLOGICAL LEVEL

On this level there is a need to investigate the electrical functioning of the brain and, of course, a full E.E.G. report is necessary. Even more important than an electroencephalographic record is an investigation of the child's motor functioning. It is now possible, as Prechtl[16] has done using a portable E.E.G. machine, to obtain electropolymyographs which will help determine any muscle dysfunction which is attributable to neurological dysfunction. A useful test of finger agnosia is that suggested by Kinsbourne and Warrington[17] as it will pick up any tactile or haptic deficits in the hand and fingers.

The muscles of the eyes can be evaluated for normal functioning by using electrodes to obtain oculomotor tracings. By this means, any choreiform (twitching) or irregular eye movements will be detected. On the broader motor level there is always the Lincoln Oseretsky Motor Performance Scale (I have found that if one gives a few impromptu tests of body balance and finger coordination one achieves the same diagnostic objective).

Along with the above tests, assessments of the child's vision and hearing should be made by competent professional people. Apart from the usual thorough audiometry examination, a speech and hearing expert should evaluate the child's articulation, re-check his auditory discrimination and even administer a language assessment scale. Learning disability personnel can utilize the services of suitably trained speech and hearing people particularly in the diagnosis and remediation of articulation and listening-auditory deficits.

THE TECHNIQUE OF "FUNNELING-IN"

Although each child will probably require more than ten hours of testing and other examinations, there is no need to extend the procedure indefinitely. It is a useful practice to look at the information yielded by the Family Information Form, the W.I.S.C., the I.T.P.A., the Frostig, and Auditory Discrimination Test with a view to discovering those areas in which the child functions well and those in which he appears to have broad deficits. For example, if he successfully completes the Frostig and spatial items on the W.I.S.C. and I.T.P.A., there will be no need to give him any further visuospatial tests such as the Beery or Memory-for-Designs. However, assuming his auditory functioning to be poor, there may be a need to investigate the problem in more detail using such tests as Melody Discrimination, and Articulation Assessment. Referral to the speech and hearing clinic might be advisable. When funneling-in on a deficit, it is better to give too many tests than too few.

CROSS-ANALYSIS AND CONSISTENT PATTERNING

Once all the test results and other information are at hand, all should be written up on a large chalk-board in separate chalk-drawn cells until the board looks like a vast mosaic. One then cross-analyzes all the figures and information searching for consistent patterns and profiles which will delineate precisely the areas of both dysfunction and sound performance on each of the four levels. Usually two or more people from the team, including the psychologist and educator, should carry through this cross-analysis.

THE DIAGNOSTIC REPORT FORM

The diagnostic coordinator next draws up a rather precise summary of these deficits, and he does so under each of the four headings: the Academic Levels, the Cognitive/Sensorimotor Level, the Personality/Emotional/Motivational Level, and the Neurophysiological Level. Underneath these is a space for further comment on etiology, interlevel complications, suspected compound deficits, and any other important special points in the child's background such as parental or sibling suicide, *known* brain damage, and multiple births.

The sheet which is used for setting out the remedial prescriptions follows closely the one used for the diagnostic report. In other words, a prescription is written for each of the several levels in which defects have been identified, and if there is no prescription for any particular level there should be entered in its place an explanation of why remediation is not necessary. As on the diagnostic sheet, there is space under the various remedial prescriptions for further comment, in which detailed explanation of the choice of remedial topics, techniques, and other teaching ideas and devices can be entered.

MULTITRACK REMEDIATION

Normally several remedial or training tracks of learning on several levels will be in progress during the first half of the child's total time spent in tuition be it days, weeks, or months. Once the respective remedial objectives have been achieved, the individual tracks along which the child is progressing may be either slowly phased out or merged together as tuition progresses. For example, a child with a severe visuospatial problem may require on the academic level a considerable amount of (1) writing and (2) reading of large-print stories. Once the child has mastered writing, the two tracks would merge into a program of writing down summaries of stories he has read. The same child on the sensorimotor level may also have embarked initially on a Frostig Program of Developmental Perception, a task which might take up another ten minutes of his lesson time each day. If the child were poorly motivated some high interest technique might be used, such as utilizing a boy's interest in racing cars as a theme for most of his academic work. On the neurophysiological level, the child might be given yet another learning track, for example, the training of eye-hand coordination on suitable (and one would hope enjoyable) apparatus.

As the child progressed along each of these tracks, they would in turn be phased out or merged until all were coalesced into one or two programs on the academic level. In most cases of reading disability these would obviously include reading, writing, and spelling. Similar multitrack programs can and should be devised for other learning disabilities, for example, in mathematics.

DIAGNOSTIC REMEDIATION

The diagnosis of learning disabilities does not stop with the onset of remediation. In fact, continuous diagnostic remediation should be practiced, with the teacher prepared to modify her procedures as the need arises. I have invented the phrase "track advancement effectors" to describe the often unitary occasions, contingencies, situations, devices, actions, ideas, insights, steps, modifications, rearrangements, and inventions which cause the child to move nearer the academic cognitive/sensorimotor, social, neurological, and physiological objectives which will have been suggested in the multitrack prescription for remediation. The teacher should watch for these track advancement effectors because they will help her structure future remediation for both the child in hand and other learning disability cases.

Task analysis is a valuable technique in the process of diagnostic remediation. Each step of each lesson on each level should be examined before and after the remedial session for the purpose of isolating unit-deficits within the immediate tasks. This seems time-consuming, but the overall result may be a considerable shortening of the entire program.

Since this is a paper primarily devoted to an overall description of diagnostic procedures and techniques, it is not the place to elaborate further on the valuable remedial technique of task analysis or the many other possible methods of remediation. I have described many of these elsewhere.[18]

REFERENCES

1. Neale, Marie D.: *Neale Analysis of Reading Ability.* London, Macmillan, 1964.
2. Spalding, R. B. and Spalding: *The Writing Road to Reading.* New York, Morrow, 1962.
3. Bannatyne, A. D.: The Etiology of Dyslexia and the Color Phonics System. Paper (Published 1967) presented at the Third Annual Conference of the Association for Children with Learning Disabilities, Tulsa, March 1966.
4. Kirk, S. A.: *The Illinois Test of Psycholinguistic Abilities* (Rev. Ed.) Urbana, Illinois University, 1968.
5. Frostig, Marianne: *Developmental Test of Visual Perception.* Palo Alto, Consulting Psychologists, 1964.
6. Graham, F. K. and Kendall, B. S.: *Memory-For-Designs Test.* Psychological Test Specialists, Box 1441, Missoula, Montana, 1960.
7. Beery, K. E. and Buktenica, N.: *Berry-Buktenica Developmental Test of Visual-Motor Integration (VMI).* Chicago, Follett, 1967.
8. Wepman, J.: *Wepman Auditory Discrimination Test.* Chicago, Chicago Language Research, 1958.
9. Drake, Charles: *P.E.R.C. Auditory Discrimination Test.* Wellesley, Perceptual and Educational Research Center, 1966.
10. Wolf, Clifton, W.: An experimental investigation of specific language disability (Dyslexia). *Bulletin Orton Society, 17.* 1967.
11. Money, John: *Road Map Test of Direction Sense.* Baltimore, John Hopkins, 1966.
12. Benton, A. L.: *Benton Protocol for Right-Left Discrimination: Right-Left Discrimination and Finger Localization: Development and Pathology.* New York, Hoeber-Harper, 1959.
13. Harris: *Harris Test of Lateral Dominance.* New York, Psychological Corp., 1947.
14. Bene, E. and Anthony: Children's Version and Adult Version of the Family Relations Test; National Foundation for Educational Research. Upton Park, Slough, Bucks, England. The Mere, 1966.
15. Sarason, S. B. *et al.*: Test anxiety scale for children and general anxiety scale for children. In: *Anxiety in Elementary School Children.* New York, Wiley & Sons, 1960.
16. Prechil, H. F. R.: Reading difficulties as a neurological problem in childhood. In Money, J. (Ed.): *Reading Disability.* Baltimore, John Hopkins, 1962.
17. Kinsbourne, M. and Warrington, E. K.: The development of finger differentiation. *J Exp Psychol Vol. 15* (Part 2), May 1963.
18. Bannatyne, A. D.: Matching remedial methods with specific deficits. Paper (Published) presented at the 1967 International Convocation on Children and Young Adults with Learning Disabilities, Home for Crippled Children, Pittsburgh, February 1967.

SECTION C

PERCEPTUAL-MOTOR DISABILITIES

Chapter 6

PERCEPTUAL-MOTOR ASPECTS
OF LEARNING DISABILITIES

Newell C. Kephart

T HE FOLLOWING DISCUSSION outlines a portion of the rationale for dealing with the child with learning disabilities developed by the author over the past twenty-five years. It is based largely upon clinical observation of the behavior of many such children and forms the basis of the therapy program of the Achievement Center for Children, Purdue University.

Most of the learning experiences which the public school presents to the child are oriented toward symbolic materials. Visually, we present words, diagrams, and similar representations on a printed page. Verbally, we manipulate conceptual items and deal in intricate, logical sequences. Underlying such presentations is a fundamental assumption: that the child has established an adequate orientation to the basic realities of the universe, i.e. space and time. It is well known that ability to deal with symbolic and conceptual materials is based upon consistent and veridical perceptions of the environment. Numerous, normative studies have indicated that the child, under normal conditions, has established a stable world by the age of six years, when he comes to us in the public schools. Therefore, our fundamental assumption is legitimate.

However, in a significant percentage of children, accidents occur during the developmental period. The accident may be any one of a large number of events. Its effect is to interfere with the establishment of a stable perceptual-motor world. As

Reprinted from *Exceptional Children*, Vol. 31 (1964), pp. 201-206. By permission of the author and publisher.

a result, many children come into our school system lacking the fundamental assumptions which underlie so much of the material which we present.

For the child who has been unable to establish the three dimensions of Euclidean space in his visual world, the words on a page of print may become an unintelligible mass of meaningless marks. They may not hold together into the compact groups, words and phrases, with which we deal. They may not hold still, but float about on the page. Worst of all, they may look different to him at different times and under different circumstances.

For the child who has been unable to establish a firm temporal dimension in his environment, the verbal discussions which we present may be no more than a meaningless jargon of sounds. Our intricate, step-by-step logical procedures may be difficult to organize without a temporal dimension along which to arrange them. Consider the difficulty which many children have in organizing the sequence of steps in long division.

For this significant percentage of children, the materials which we present in the classroom may cause difficulty, not because of the content or inability to deal with the content, but because of inability to deal with the mechanics of the presentation. Where the mechanics of the task break down, the content of necessity suffers. It may be that the child has difficulty not so much in learning to read as he has in seeing the words on the page. It may be that he has trouble not so much in understanding arithmetical reasoning as he does in organizing the steps of this reasoning in time.

ENVIRONMENTAL INTERACTIONS

The child's first interactions with his environment are motor. His first learnings are motor learnings. His first attempts to organize the environment are based upon these motor interactions. For a very large number of children, the learning difficulty begins at this early motor stage. He learned to use his motor responses to accomplish certain ends, but he failed to expand or generalize these motor responses so that they formed the basis of information gathering. He has learned a motor response for a specific end, but has not developed a motor interaction with his environment.

The difference here is between a motor skill and a motor pattern. A motor skill is a motor act which may be performed with high degrees of precision. However, it is limited in extent; it is designed for a specific result, and only limited variation is possible. The motor pattern, on the other hand, involves lesser degrees of precision, but greater degrees of variability. Its purpose is much broader, and extensive variation is possible.

Consider the difference between walking as a motor skill and walking as a part of a locomotor pattern. The young child first develops a walking skill. He learns how to maintain an upright position while he puts one foot in front of the other. This process allows him to move from point A to point B. However, most of his attention must be devoted to the motor process itself, what part must move and how it must move. Very little attention can be devoted to the purpose of the movement. The skill is very limited and little variation is possible. Thus, if he encounters an obstacle in moving from point A to point B, he may well have to stop and give up the entire task. He cannot veer around the obstacle or step over it because these adjustments involve greater variation than his limited skill will permit.

Consider, on the other hand, the locomotor pattern of the older child. He can get from point A to point B by any one of a number of specific skills. He can walk, run, skip, jump, and so on. If an obstacle looms in his way, he can veer around or go over or under it as the problem demands. In all of these extensive variations, he does not need to expend attention on the motor act itself. This act has been generalized; it is no longer specific. As a result, he can shift directions or shift movement sequences without undue attention to the process itself.

With the walking skill the child is limited to rather specific purposes and ends. The process does not involve a continuous, changing, viable relationship with the environment. Only through a locomotor pattern can the child maintain a consistent, uninterrupted interaction with the environment surrounding him. The development of a stable body of information about this environment demands such a continuous, reliable interaction.

Thus motor patterns become essential for information gathering at this basic early stage in the development of the world of the child.

There are four of these motor patterns which appear to be of particular significance to us in the field of education.

1. *Balance and maintenance of posture.* All spatial relationships in the world about us are relative. Right and left, up and down, behind and before are relationships which are not given directly by perceptual data. They develop out of the observation and organization of relationships between objects. A well organized system of such relationships will include the three Euclidean dimensions of space. All of these relationships, however, are relative. Each object is related to each other object, and there is no objective direction. The child must systematize this set of relationships through the learning resulting from his interaction with the objects in his environment.

The point of origin for all such relationships is the force of gravity. It, therefore, becomes important for the child to establish a relationship to the force of gravity and to be able to maintain this relationship and the awareness of the center of gravity throughout all of his activiites. It is only through a constant and stable relationship to gravity that a point of origin for spatial relationships can be established. This stable relationship to gravity is achieved through the motor pattern of balance and posture. By maintaining the relationship of his body to the force of gravity, the child identifies the direction of the line of gravity and maintains this constant throughout his interactions with the environment.

The child should be able to maintain his balance and relationship to gravity under many conditions and with his body in a large number of different positions. He should not lose balance or lose his awareness of gravity when the position of his body changes or when its motion alters. On the other hand, his relationship to gravity should be variable so that he can maintain this relationship under a large number of conditions. His balance and posture should be dynamic and fluid rather than rigid. It is only through such a dynamic relationship to gravity that a continuous awareness of its direction can be maintained.

2. *Locomotion.* The locomotor skills are those motor activities which move the body through space, i.e. walking, running, jumping, skipping, hopping, and rolling. It is with the pattern of locomotion that the child investigates the relationships within the space around him. By moving his body from one point to another, he learns to appreciate the properties of this surrounding space and the relationships between the objects in it. Out of such knowledge a space world with stable coordinates will develop. Locomotor skills should be variable. They should permit the child to divert his attention from the movement itself to the purpose of the movement. They should permit the child to adjust to changes in the environment and to obstacles which may lie in the path of his movement.

3. *Contact.* The contact skills are those motor activities with which the child manipulates objects. Involved are the skills of reach, grasp, and release. It is with the contact skills that the child investigates through manipulation the relationships within objects. In order to obtain this information, he must be able to reach out and make contact with the object, he must be able to maintain this contact through grasp until he has obtained the necessary information, and he must be able to terminate this contact through release and move on to the next object. From the knowledge so gained, form perception and figure-ground relationships will develop.

The skills of reach, grasp, and release should be established well enough so that the child can divert his attention from the motor acts to the manipulation. They should also be sufficiently variable to permit him to make complex manipulations in search of information.

4. *Receipt and propulsion.* With the skills of locomotion, the child has investigated the relationships in the space around him. With the skills of contact, he has investigated the relationships within an object. However, many of the problem situations with which he must deal involve the movement of objects in space. It is with the skills of receipt and propulsion that he investigates movements in space.

Receipt skills involve those activities by which the child makes contact with a moving object. Such skills include not only the pursuit of the moving object but also the interposition of the body or parts of the body in the path of the moving object, as in catching. The skills of propulsion involve those activities by which the child impairs movement to an object. Included are throwing and batting and the more continuous skills of pushing and pulling.

Through the use of these four motor patterns, the child investigates the vast array of relationships in the environment around him. Out of this investigation he puts together a system of these relationships. The initial information is motor. It comes from the interaction through movement of the child with his environment. To develop a system, however, these interactions must be extensive, and they must be consistent. If the interactions are not sufficiently extensive, the system will not be insufficiently inclusive. If the interactions are inconsistent so that the observed relationships are not stable, the development of a system is impossible. To develop such extensive and consistent investigations, motor patterns as opposed to motor skills are required. Therefore, we are not interested in whether or not the child can walk; we are interested in whether or not he can locomote in order to obtain information about objects in space. We are interested in a sort of motor generalization by which the repertory of movements available to the child, whatever they may be, are used for the purpose of gathering information about the environment around him.

Many children find the motor learning required for a learning pattern difficult. As a result, they stop with a motor skill. They require additional help and additional learning experiences to continue this motor learning until a level is reached which will permit the use of movement, not only for specific purposes but for the more generalized purpose of information gathering. It becomes the responsibility of the public schools to offer this aid and to help the child expand his motor learning.

DIRECTIONAL RELATIONSHIPS

Out of these motor investigations of the environment comes a system of relationships. At this point the system is primarily a motor system. It exists with the child's own body. The directions of space are beginning to develop, but they are limited to the movement relationships which occur in his body. The vertical direction has developed and stabilized out of his use of balance and posture. Out of his more extensive motor activities he has developed a laterality among his own movements. He now knows when a movement is on the right side of the body and when it is on the left; and he knows how far to the right or how far to the left it may be. He has developed a sort of a right-left gradient within his own movement system.

For further progress, however, this system of directional relationships must be transferred to outside objects. Since he cannot investigate all of the objects in his environment, in a motor fashion, he must learn to investigate them perceptually. These perceptual data, however, do not at this point possess the spatial relationships which his motor data possess. Perceptual data come to have such relationships by projecting motor information onto perceptual information.

It is through the perceptual-motor match that the child makes this projection. As he manipulates an object or relationship motorwise, he observes the perceptual data which he is concurrently receiving and particularly observes changes in these perceptual data. Through a matching of the motor data and the perceptual data, he is given the same information. Now perceived objects have a right and a left, just as manipulated objects have a right and left. He can *see* up and down, just as he previously learned to *feel* up and down. Through this projection process, the perceptual world comes to be systematized and organized in the same fashion as the motor world was organized. It is only through such a projection that a veridical organization of the perceptual world is possible.

Important here is the control of the external sense organs. The sensory avenue which gives us the greatest amount of information and is most subject to control is that of vision. The visual information is controlled by the direction in which the eyes are pointed. The pointing of the eyes, in turn, is controlled by the extraocular muscles. The child must learn to explore an object with his eyes in the same way in which he previously explored it with his hands. It is important, however, that the exploration with the eyes duplicates the exploration with the hands, and that the resulting information matches the earlier information.

Two problems arise at this point. First of all, the child must must learn to manipulate his eyes through the development of patterns of movement in the extraocular muscles. A second, and perhaps more important problem, is that of learning to manipulate the eyes in terms of the incoming information. The only way in which the child can know that his eyes are under control is to evaluate their information. The criterion of ocular control is the visual information which results. However, the child is only now developing a stable visual world with which to evaluate the present perception. Therefore, the body of information which should provide the criterion for ocular control is not yet present. On the other hand, without ocular control the incoming contributions to the body of visual information are inconsistent and spotty. Thus, the control of his eyes is hampered by his lack of a stable visual world while, at the same time, the stability of his visual world is impaired by his lack of ocular control.

The solution to this dilemma is in motor manipulation. The child investigates motorwise. He then experiments with the movement of his eyes until it gives him information which matches his motor information. Since the body of motor information is reasonably stable, he stabilizes the visual information when a match occurs. Through many such experiments, he develops a visual world which duplicates his motor world. He has established a perceptual-motor match. When this match is adequate, he can drop out the intervening motor manipulation and use his now stable visual information to control his eyes and thus control new visual input. Now all information—motor or perceptual, sensory input or motor response—is a part of a stable overall system which gives consistent information wherever it is tapped. Control of both perceptual information and motor response is possible and both are a part of one consistent system.

It is obvious that such learning will be difficult and will require extensive experimentation. Here again the learning process frequently breaks down with the result that an adequate match between perceptual information and motor information is not accomplished. For such children there is limited stability in the perceptual world. They cannot see the relationships of right-left, up-down, and so on. For them, the letters on our page do not present a stable directional relationship. If you cannot see a difference between right and left, it is very difficult to distinguish between a "b" and a "d." If you do not see a difference between up and down, it is easy to confuse a "b" and a "p." Thus, for such children the mechanics of the reading task become extremely difficult. To deal with our symbolic material, the child requires a stable spatial world. Such a world can be established only through the development of a system of spatial relationships learned first in the motor activities of the child and later projected onto perceptual data. Such a system must be both generalized and extensive.

OTHER RELATIONSHIPS

The behavior of the child occurs not only in space but also in time. For this reason there is another dimension of behavior which must be generalized and systematized. This is the temporal dimension. There are three aspects of time which are important to us in education: synchrony, rhythm, and sequence.

The basis of temporal judgments arises through synchrony. The child must first be able to appreciate simultaneity in time before he can appreciate serial events in time. Synchrony is the point of origin of the temporal dimension.

Having developed a point of origin through synchrony, the child requires a temporal scale. This scale must be characterized by stable, equal intervals. Rhythm provides such a scale, and it is through rhythm that he can estimate and evaluate temporal intervals.

Sequencing is the ordering of events in time. It is obvious that such ordering is difficult or impossible unless there is a temporal scale upon which to superimpose this order. Unless the child can appreciate temporal intervals it is difficult to organize events in terms of their temporal relationships.

As with the relationships in space, relationships in time also developed first in the motor activities of the child. Synchrony is observed when muscles move in concert. Rhythm is developed when muscles move alternately or recurrently. Sequence is observed when movements occur in coordinated patterns. From the generalization of many such observations, a temporal system evolves, and a temporal dimension develops.

This motor-temporal system must then be projected onto outside events just as the motor-spatial system was projected onto the perception of outside objects. Auditory rhythm develops and speech begins to be rhythmical. The eyes move rhythmically across a page of print preserving the temporal relationships of the material as well as the spatial relationships. Now the step by step procedures of logical reasoning can be organized in time.

When these two systems are adequate, the child can translate activities from one to another. Consider the task of drawing. The child first looks at the copy. His visual perception gives him a simultaneous spatial presentation of the material. As he begins to draw, however, he must translate this simultaneous spatial impression into a series of events in time which will preserve the continuity and relationships of the whole. If the copy is a square, for example, he must translate the four simultaneously presented lines into a series of directional movements performed one at a time but resulting in a square form.

As in the development of spatial relationships, many children experience difficulty in the development of a temporal relationship. As a result, they have difficulty organizing events in time, and they have particular difficulty with our educational materials in which temporal sequence is vital. We must be prepared to aid these children in the development of a temporal dimension of behavior.

CONCLUSION

Since the materials and activities which we present in the public school are so frequently highly symbolically oriented, we have a tendency to look primarily at the child's symbolic response and at the symbolic aspects of his performance. Perhaps our preoccupation with symbolic variables has blinded us to the more fundamental problems of many children. It is possible that their orientation to the physical universe which surrounds them is disturbed. It is possible that, as a result of this disturbance, their difficulties are not so much with the content of our activities as with the mechanics involved. Greater attention to the child's methods of handling the mechanics of our tasks might result in less frustration for us and more learning for the child.

REFERENCES

1. Bartley, S. A.: *Principles of Perception.* New York, Harper and Brothers, 1958.
2. Gessell, A., Ilg, Florence A., and Bullis, G. E.: *Vision—Its Development in Infant and Child.* New York, Hoeber Medical Division, Harper and Row, 1941.
3. Jersild, A. T.: *Child Psychology.* Englewood Cliffs, Prentice-Hall, 1954.
4. Kephart, N. C.: *The Slow Learner in the Classroom.* Columbus. C. E. Merrill, 1960.
5. Kephart, N. C.: *The Brain Injured Child in the Classroom.* Chicago. National Society for Crippled Children and Adults, 1963.
6. Kephart, N. C.: Perceptual-motor correlates of education. In Kirk, S. A. and Becker, W. (Ed.). *Conference on Children with Minimal Brain Impairments.* Urbana, Univ. of Illinois, 1963, pp. 13-25.
7. Piaget, J., and Inhelder, B.: *The Child's Conception of Space.* London, Routledge and Kegan Paul, 1956.
8. Small, V. H.: Ocular pursuit abilities and readiness for reading. Unpublished masters thesis, Purdue Univ., 1958.
9. Strauss, A. A., and Lehtinen, Laura E.: *Psychopathology and Education of the Brain Injured Child.* New York, Grune and Stratton, 1947, Vol. 1.
10. Strauss, A. A., and Kephart, N .C.: *Psychopathology and Education of the Brain Injured Child.* New York, Grune and Stratton, 1955, Vol. 2.

Chapter 7

PERCEPTUAL-MOTOR TRAINING
AND BASIC ABILITIES

GEORGE H. EARLY and THEODORE M. SHARPE

T HE TYPICAL CHILD whom we see at the Purdue Achievement Center for Children is there for one main reason: He cannot adequately cope with the academic demands of the school. As we evaluate this child, we usually find that certain basic abilities are impaired or dysfunctional or operating inefficiently. Each child is different, and each has his own pattern of strengths and weaknesses. Our usual findings, however, are that the difficulties are fundamental ones.

Our typical child has problems in organizing the elements of his environment and in making flexible and efficient responses to that environment. The world out there does not "hold together" consistently for him. The key elements of space or time, or both, often are unstable for him, and the varieties of instability are almost endless. As we look at the child himself (using a variety of standardized measures and clinical evaluation techniques), we often find that he lacks an adequate internal organization of himself and his information-processing channels. We believe there is a connection between a child's internal organization of himself and his ability to organize his environment; a child organizes his world by projecting his internal organization of himself outward upon his world. Thus, if he has basic deficiencies in his own internal organization, we would expect corresponding deficiencies in his organization of the world in which he must function.

With this point of view, we try to discover the basic problems

Reprinted from the *Academic Therapy Quarterly*, Vol. 5 (1970), pp. 235-240.
By permission of the authors and publisher.

of internal organization, to help the child develop a better organization, and to help him project his organization more efficiently on to the environment. Our preliminary goal is to discover the basic difficulties and to build stronger basic abilities. These newly strengthened basic abilities must then be generalized to academic tasks.

This point of view is receiving widespread attention from educators and other professionals who deal with children. The present state of our knowledge in this area is such that we try to avoid making dogmatic pronouncements, realizing that our assertions are tentative at best, and that there is a crying need for more and better research. The business of research involves, among other things, observing and then making hypotheses from our observations. In a recent case, we obtained some interesting results which led us to some hypotheses. The results and hypotheses follow.

John (fictitious name) was first seen for initial evaluation in January 1969. (The initial evaluation is a four-day period of evaluation, parent education, and development of a home training program.) At the time of initial evaluation, John's age was nine years and nine months. He was seen for reevaluation in May and again in October 1969, and he is still a client of the Purdue Achievement Center. (Reevaluation is a one-day period for determining progress and making indicated changes in the home training program.)

John's parents are intelligent and perceptive people, both college graduates, with the father serving in a professional capacity. During the initial evaluation, they reported the following about John: hyperactivity, tension when performing, generally achievement oriented with considerable internal pressure to perform adequately, behavior problems in general, twitching, "complete breakdown" in first grade (i.e. an inability to cope with demands of school, rather than an emotional breakdown), rigid structure of daily routines, hesitance in participating in sports, inadequate peer relationships, and academic grades generally at an acceptable level but achieved only by struggling.

In general, our initial evaluation indicated intellectual functioning at high-average level, difficulty in visual-motor, visual-memory, and visual-sequencing areas, inadequate body differentiation and gross motor coordination, and a general inability to perform rhythmical gross motor movements. John's writing was a "splinter skill" and required inordinate cognitive processing to perform the writing task.* His reading performance was characterized by looking back and forth, determining meaning from contextual clues, substitution of words, and a general lack of rhythm and flow of vocal responses in oral reading. Silent reading comprehension and listening comprehension were markedly lower than oral reading comprehension.

Based on these findings, a home training program was prescribed. Along with the home training, recommendations to the school were made. The home training program was built around efforts to improve the basic deficits noted on the initial evaluation. Recommendations to the school included suggestions to reduce external visual stimulation, utilize the stronger auditory channel in learning, reduce temporarily the demands for visual-motor performance (writing), examine John orally wherever possible, work for a generally reduced pressure for performance, and develop an enhanced ego strength.

Three of the standard measures that were obtained on initial evaluation and subsequent reevaluations are of special interest as indicators of progress. These are the Wechsler Intelligence Scale for Children (WISC), the Illinois Test of Psycholinguistic Abilities (ITPA), and the Durrell Analysis of Reading Difficulty. All three measures (among others) were administered during initial evaluation in January 1969. The Durrell was readministered during the May reevaluation, and the WISC and ITPA were readministered during the October reevaluation. Thus, test-retest comparisons can be made in this case. Tables 7-I, 7-II, and 7-III show results obtained.

One of the authors of this paper (Sharpe) was the examiner for each WISC and each ITPA; hence, intertester differences are not a factor. In view of elapsed time between test and retest, we

---

* See Early, George H.: Developing perceptual-motor skills: overburdened cognitive processes. *Academic Therapy*, 5:59-62, Fall 1969.

TABLE 7-I

DURRELL ANALYSIS OF READING DIFFICULTY

Item	Grade Equivalents	
	January 1969	May 1969
Oral reading comprehension	7	7
Silent reading comprehension	4H*	6M**
Listening comprehension	3	6
Flash words	6M	No retest
Word analysis	6M	No retest
Visual memory for words	4	6

* H indicates high part of grade level.
** M indicates middle of grade level.

TABLE 7-II

WECHSLER INTELLIGENCE SCALE FOR CHILDREN

Item	January 1969		October 1969	
	Raw Score	Scaled Score	Raw Score	Scaled Score
Verbal:				
Information	16	14	16	13
Comprehension	14	13	13	11
Arithmetic	8	10	9	10
Similarities	14	15	13	14
Vocabulary	39	14	38	12
Digit span	10	12	9	9
Performance:				
Picture completion	7	6	11	10
Picture arrangement	31	12	32	12
Block design	34	14	33	13
Object assembly	24	13	24	12
Coding	34	10	52	16
I.Q. scores are as follows:				
Verbal I.Q.		119		110
Performance I.Q.		107		118
Full-Scale I.Q.		115		115

TABLE 7-III

ILLINOIS TEST OF PSYCHOLINGUISTIC ABILITIES

January 1969	Language Age (Yrs. and Mos.)	October 1969	Language Age (Yrs. and Mos.)
Auditory decoding	+8-10	Auditory reception	10-2
Visual decoding	+8-9	Visual reception	7-9
Auditory-vocal association	+9-0	Auditory association	+10-11
Visual-motor association	8-7	Visual association	9-4
Vocal encoding	6-11	Verbal expression	9-1
Motor encoding	+8-8	Manual expression	+10-4
Auditory-vocal automatic	8-9	Grammatic closure	+10-4
		Visual closure	+10-6
Auditory-vocal sequential	+8-6	Auditory memory	+10-3
Visual-motor sequential	9-0	Visual memory	+10-5

The experimental edition was administered in January, and the revised edition was administered in October.

believe the results are valid. After retest, the following examiner comments (WISC and ITPA) were recorded, and are considered significant.

WISC

(Comment on the sharp increase in Picture Completion and Coding subtests)

Not only do we see increases in scores, but there are also qualitative differences. Eye-hand coordination has definitely improved. In the January Coding subtest (which requires use of paper and pencil) the lines were dark, heavy, and labored; in October, the performance was smooth and flexible. In the October Picture Completion subtest, the responses were smooth and efficient; this was not true of the January performance. Taken together, the picture completion and coding subtests indicate that visual perception of detail and the ability to organize detail have improved significantly.

ITPA

Though the two tests are not identical, some conclusions may be drawn on the basis of age norms.*

---

* In January, the experimental form of the ITPA was administered; then in October, the recently standardized form of the ITPA was used.

Visuoperceptual and visual-motor abilities appear to have increased beyond that expected on the basis of time lapsed between tests. Verbal expression is presently within the normal range, while it was weak at the previous testing. Manual expression is presently above average, while it was previously average. John's ability to receive information has weakened slightly, which may reflect a lack of emphasis in this area and implies a need for language stimulation and enrichment.

In general, the profile indicates progress in perceptual and expressive areas and a gain in self-confidence.

In October, reports from parents and teachers, together with our own clinical observations, indicated the following: a marked decrease in hyperactivity, improved concentration, more ready participation in school activities, and improved homework. There is an overall impression that John is becoming more sure of himself; that his self-image is improving. Math continues to be a vexing problem. While we see general improvement in motor and perceptual-motor functioning, residual problems in differentiation and motor and visual-motor rhythm are noted.

In assessing John's gains as indicated on the three standard measures (Durrell, WISC, ITPA), we note that these instruments indicate significant gains in the basic areas of visual perception, visual memory, and visual-motor coordinaton. The WISC and ITPA generally are thought to tap fairly basic abilities, and the above significant gains are indicated by these instruments. The Durrell Analysis is oriented more to achievement, and it is interesting to note that gains on this instrument are mainly in those areas that one would expect from gains on the WISC and the ITPA. On the Durrell, both Silent Reading Comprehension and Visual Memory for Words showed significant gains, such gains being logically associated with those on the WISC and ITPA, i.e. Visual Perception, Visual Memory, and Visual-Motor Coordination. (Notice that the Visual Memory for Words on the Durrell requires a visual-motor or written response at the level used during both administrations of this instrument.)

We suggest that our training program is the major factor in the significant gains noted in the basic areas of visual perception, visual memory, and visual-motor coordination. We suggest further that the gains noted are in those basic areas that were preventing John from using his good intelligence in the learning process. In other words, we believe our training program has eliminated certain fundamental blocks to learning.

At this point, our story should have the typical Hollywood happy ending: John should have no more problems in school, and his academic achievement should increase by leaps and bounds. Such is not the case. Arithmetic still plagues John (and us). While reading ability is well above grade placement, he frankly (by his own statement) does not like to read. We feel that John's aversion to reading is slowing his rate of progress in those abilities tapped by the verbal portion of the WISC. A companion of the results of the two WISC administrations reveals little or no progress in several of the verbal subtests, resulting in a drop in verbal I.Q. While young children's verbal progress is dependent principally upon the verbal productions of people around them, such as parents, the older child, such as John, must must depend increasingly upon reading for the development of vocabulary and verbal skills. Thus, it seems reasonable to assume that John's lack of progress in the verbal tasks of the WISC is a result of his aversion to reading. John's lack of progress in the verbal area stands in contrast to the rather dramatic improvements found in other basic areas. How can we explain this?

From all the information available to us, we think something like this is happening: Some of John's basic problems in learning have been remedied to the point where we could expect a more advanced level of academic performance. When John approaches academic tasks, however, old habits still prevail. In arithmetic, we feel he is inhibited by past failures and, therefore, does not utilize fully his present higher basic abilities. In reading, he tends to utilize his old inefficient approaches and does not employ his new and improved basic abilities to the fullest advantage.

Put another way, we believe our training program is improving certain basic abilities that are fundamental to the learning task; however, at present these enhanced abilities have not completely transferred over to the maximum academic achievement that we would expect. The transfer is, to some extent, impeded by John's old habits of learning. Our present training is based upon an attempt to break through these old and inefficient approaches to learning and to bring into play the new and improved basic abilities, working all the while to increase still further those same basic abilities.

While John's performance is impeded by his old, unnecessary work habits, he is similarly adversely affected by his old attitudes about himself and about tasks such as reading. It must be remembered that this is an achievement-oriented child who has previously proven to himself that tasks such as reading are difficult, if not impossible for him, and are at least annoying. Thus, old attitudes as well as old habits must be seen by John as inappropriate, and he must realize that he can apply his new skills to these tasks. Therefore, in all our efforts we are deliberately trying to avoid pressuring John or making him the victim of overly enthusiastic, "accelerated" techniques.

John, then, quite possibly is in a transitional stage, a stage where perceptual-motor training has produced gains in basic abilities, yet still a stage where transfer of basic abilities has not been accomplished completely. We think this may be an extremely important stage that has not received the professional attention it deserves. The whole subject of perceptual-motor training is still somewhat controversial. Furious discussions are swirling around the subject, producing at present more heat than light. It is this transitional stage that typically seems to be ignored. A case in point is the recent series of studies by S. Alan Cohen.* In addition to several basic procedural questions that we would raise in connection with Cohen's studies, we suggest that he has completely ignored what we have called the transitional stage. That is, once basic abilities have been developed or improved, there logically should be a stage where efforts are made to promote transfer of these abilities over to appropriate levels of academic achievement.

From our experiences with John and hundreds of children with

---

* Cohen, Alan S.: Studies in visual perception and reading in disadvantaged children. *Journal of Learning Disabilities* 2: (No. 10), October 1969.

similar problems, we would state the following hypotheses, none of which are original with us.

1. For a significant number of children, inadequate academic achievement stems from certain inadequate abilities that are basic to the learning task.

2. For a significant number of children, proper remediation can increase significantly those lagging basic abilities that seem to be essential to efficient learning.

3. When abilities basic to academic learning must be instituted in order to assure the successful transfer of skills to academic achievement. We cannot assume that this transfer will be realized automatically when we consider the persistence of old attitudes and habits.

We urge the testing of these hypotheses by appropriate research.

REFERENCES

1. Durrell, Donald D.: *Durrell Analysis of Reading Difficulty.* New York, Harcourt, Brace and World, 1955.
2. Kirk, Samuel A., and McCarthy, James J.: *Illinois Test of Psycholinguistic Abilities.* Urbana. Univ. of Illinois, 1968.
3. Wechsler, David I.: *Wechsler Intelligence Scale for Children.* New York, Psychological Corp., 1949.

Chapter 8

AN HISTORICAL PERSPECTIVE
TO PHYSIOLOGICAL EDUCATION

Miriam Sper Magdol

T HE CURRENT EXPLOSION of interest in mentally retarded, brain-damaged, and slow-learning children has brought with it a new, yet old, approach to their training. From varied sources one hears of research and experimentation that boldly approaches teaching in terms of movement organization and/or sense training. Marianne Frostig discusses perceptual training; Carl Delacato speaks of the prevention of reading problems; Newell C. Kephart deals with methods for the slow learner; G. N. Getman writes about training intelligence; Ray H. Barsch speaks of organizing the processing modalities. Although the terminology and emphases differ, all of these theorists deal with psychological education.

The philosophical roots of physiological education are to be found in the sense empiricism of John Locke. Because of Locke the attention of the educator shifted, for the first time, from training the faculties to training the senses. Abandoning notions of inborn capacities and a common human nature, he developed his *tabula rasa* theory of the human mind and claimed that the environment supplied all knowledge through the senses. This led to a reevaluation of the assumption that mental deficiency was incurable. Locke's medical background helped him to see each pupil as a patient, hence as a unique individual: each needed specific kinds of attention; each needed specific kinds of help.

Locke's investigations were based on adult needs rather than

Reprinted from the *Academic Therapy Quarterly*, Vol. 3 (1969), pp. 162-170. By permission of the author and publisher.

childhood capacities. This circumstance may explain his failure to deal with the training of the senses as such. At one point he does indicate that the senses are "beholden to experience, improvement, and acquired notions," but this seems to be as close as he came to dealing with the early development of sensation (quoted from Locke's *Essay*).[1, p. 24]

No educational theorist since Locke has been able to ignore his great contribution. All subsequent theories of education have some base in his works. His theory was diverse, however, and it was inevitable that later thinkers would be influenced by varied aspects of his philosophy.

Rousseau accepted and enlarged upon Locke's concept of individuality. He, too, adjusted education to the child. He gave consideration to differences due to the individual, to age, to sex, and to race. In addition, he postulated stages of mental growth. In childhood the intellect is developed only through the senses. In *Emile* he says:

> At the commencement of life, when memory and imagination are as yet inactive, the child limits his attention to what actually affects his senses. He wants to touch and handle everything. Do not check his restlessness. This is a necessary part of his training. It is by looking, fingering, and hearing, and above all by comparing sight and touch, that he learns to feel the heat and cold, the hardness and softness, the heaviness and lightness of bodies and to judge of their size and form and all their physical properties.

Referring to movement, Rousseau says, "It is only by movement that we learn that there are things other than ourselves, and only by our own movement that we get the idea of space" (from Boyd's translation of *Emile*).[1, p. 52]

Rousseau believed that if the child were left free to play, to interact with his environment and with his peers, his motor development would come naturally. But the senses had to be deliberately trained, not just to be increasingly sensitive, but to discriminate between objects and thus be useable to exert judgment. Rousseau suggested that although the senses interact in life situations each must be trained individually. He trained the sense of touch by isolating it. He trained vision in conjunction with other senses so that what was seen could be verified.

Rousseau limits exclusive sense training to early childhood. He projects a mental element that works when the senses are active but in a manner that depends on its own properties. The educator "helps from without a process of growth which has its impulses from within, and only succeeds when he understands and respects its laws." In adolescence the child begins to reason, and the educator spends less and less time on the training of the mind.

Condillac accepted Locke's concept that sense impressions are the source of all knowledge. He added another sense impression, namely, the mental sensation of the relationship of sensations. Condillac saw no need to deliberately train the senses but did suggest that they are trained in infancy.

Pereire, in his work with deaf mutes, claimed that all sensations are a modification of the tactual. He rigorously trained the sense of touch, considering this to be basic to all other learning. According to Seguin, Pereire saw all ideas originating in the senses, felt that senses strengthen each other, felt that senses could be substituted for each other.

The most well known of the sensationalists, Jean Marc Itard, was the first to develop an elaborate, organized system of sense training. In his attempt to teach Victor, a "wild boy" found in the woods at about twelve years of age, he worked on the training of vision, hearing, voice, smell, and touch. His elaborate and still impressive goals for Victor, however, did not include a time table reflecting a maturation sequence.

Victor progressed in the areas of touch, taste, and smell fairly quickly, but vision and hearing were trained much more slowly and with far less success. Eventually Itard[2] suggested that the former are a "modification of the organ of skin" while the latter are subjective and, "enclosed in a most complicated physical apparatus, are subject to other laws and ought in some measure to form a separate class."

Itard's methods included many that are still in use. In his "Historical Review of the Treatment of the Retarded", Lloyd Dunn says: "Recently I reread Itard's reports. While 150 years old, they are as modern as tomorow. His creative and systematic approach to learning warrants reappraisal as to appropriate teaching techniques for training our severely retarded boys and girls."[3]

A basic technique of Itard's included training from gross to fine. He developed discrimination by beginning with strong contrasts and working toward finer and finer differentiation. He accomplished this goal with the use of color, size, and shape comparisons, sound discrimination, and texture contrasts. He tried to motivate by creating new needs and occasionally by introducing strong emotional stimuli. Itard greatly emphasized the role of imitation, particularly in the early years.

One of Itard's significant conclusions was that medicine must help the goals of education by "detecting the organic and intellectual peculiarities of each individual and determining therefore what education ought to do for him and what society can expect of him."

Despite Itard's feeling of failure wtih Victor, a major contribution was his rejection of the concept of incurability.

Like Itard, his pupil, Sequin, was medically oriented. It was he who first referred to part of his training method as "physiological education." "Man being a unit," writes Seguin, "is artificially analyzed, for study's sake, into his three prominent vital expressions, activity, intelligence, and will. We consider the idiot as a man infirm in the expression of his trinity. . . ." Physiological education trains the expression referred to as "activity" and simultaneously "restores the harmony of all of these functions in the young."[4]

To the sense training of Itard, Seguin adds the training of the motor system, which Rousseau claimed took care of itself. He trained first the whole system and then the parts. Whenever possible he trained with articles used in everyday life but when necessary he developed his own unique apparatus.

Seguin continually stressed the need to train and educate children to see the application of skills to daily living and for specific usage. He speaks of elevating function "to the rank of capacity." For example, when the child is being taught to grasp mechanically, the tiring exercises are terminated with a piece of cool fruit placed in each hand so that the new learning will be used in a situation that is meaningful to the child as soon as possible.

After motor training has established basic patterns Seguin trains for hand-eye coordination, the auditory sense, voice, and vision. He has the child handle objects whenever possible and thus includes tactual training. Seguin uses imitation extensively and considers it basic to learning. He trained for sensitivity to color, form, dimensions, and distance; he spoke of "intellectual deafness" and trained with three classes of sound: noises, music, and speech. Eventually he dealt with memory and imagination. He writes: ". . . the nature of the physiological training . . . is . . . not the unity of the object, but the rational comparison of objects, to be taught through any and all senses." Sensations are connected among themselves and are connected through memory with past images and new images and thus ideas are formed.

Early in the twentieth century Maria Montessori, the first woman physician in Italy, felt the influence of these early educators and developed her own didactic materials for the education of retarded children. Although her method has many other implications, sense training is a basic consideration. Montessori established a "prepared environment" in which the children were free to use materials of their own choice and at their own pace. Each of the materials was to be used in a specific manner and each provided a portion of the self-education that Montessori envisioned. The Montessori materials provide experience with length, breadth, height, color, texture, weight, size, form, and more. Montessori, like some of the modern theorists, considered sense training to be a precondition of higher intellectual functioning. "Knowledge," says Mme. Montessori's biographer, "is finding its way into those little heads *via* hands, eyes, ears, and feet."[5]

Because the methods created by the optimism and enthusiam of these early educators did not prove dramatically successful, a new trend in the education and training of the mentally retarded emerged toward the end of the nineteenth century. Although many continued to be influenced by Seguin in particular, sense training became less and less the focal point of their method.

Decroly sought to develop sensory discrimination, but also concerned himself with the relationship of the child to his family, his school, and the community. His student, Alice Desoeudres, gave much emphasis to training the senses—visual, auditory, and tactual. To this experience she added physical training, tool subjects, and moral training. She was anxious to enrich verbal expression through social activity.

Slowly, the emphasis moved to institutional care for those needing lifetime supervision, and vocational preparation for those able to remain in the community. As special classes were set up in the public schools, more and more emphasis was placed on academic skills and socialization. For a time retardates were given the same training as that given in the "normal" classroom except that the curriculum was watered down and the pace was slower.

In a small guide published in 1925, Gesell offers suggestions for teachers of normal children who have single retarded children in their classrooms. His stress is on handicrafts like knitting and weaving. In a section called Busy Work he lists activities that, he points out, are better than idleness. To some extent these suggestions provide sense training. Gesell includes such items as bead stringing, color and size sorting, cutting, tracing, and modeling. No mention is made of the value of these activities except to say that "Busy work is often educative."[6]

A brief survey of today's approach to the teaching of the mentally retarded finds that sense training is frequently incorporated but rarely stressed, and sometimes it is not even mentioned in the literature. On the whole, it is not considered fundamental to learning. In listing "special learning principles," Samuel A. Kirk gives priority to teaching in such a way as to move from the known to the unknown, to help in transfer to develop generalization, repetition, and the presentation of ideas singly and in sequence. The sixth and last principle is, "Learning is reinforced through using a variety of sense modalities—visual, vocal, auditory, kinesthetic."[7] We note that the modalities are used as reinforcers, not as preparation and foundation (as the sensationalists used them).

In Kirk and Johnson's book, sense training as such is rejected as a method of developing intelligence. "Kilpatrick," they tell us, "maintained that no sense can be improved by training. Experiments in the improvements of sense training have not supported Montessori's view."[8]

Kirk and Johnson list twelve purposes of education for the retarded. Of these, three refer to training for visual, auditory, and motor abilities, but for the most part they are interested in emotional health, academics, speech, work habits, physical health, and social adjustment. In relation to their preschool program they indicate that "more materials to work with in their play are needed for them to see, to feel, and to touch because of their lack of imagination and abstraction." But, they say, "there are few differences in motor skills between these children and normal children," therefore only the usual nursery school equipment is supplied for motor activities.

A look at the publications of the United States Department of Health, Education, and Welfare and the various state departments of education, confirms the move away from sense training and the increasing concern for the child's relationships, social competence, self-acceptance and emotional stability, ability to follow directions, and so on.

An important influence in the trend away from sensationalism is the impact of the theories of John Dewey. Like Locke, Dewey has influenced most profoundly all those educators who have followed him. Dewey's emphasis on "learning by doing" moved the stress from stimulus to response. Kolstoe suggests that the emphasis on the performance of specific skills, such as handiwork, may be traced to Dewey's urging that the learner be engaged in activities. Says Kolstoe:

> This activity approach certainly has resulted in improving the effectiveness of these youngsters. Yet the emphasis is just the opposite of that of Itard and Seguin. While Itard and Seguin were concerned with systematic presentation of stimuli, present-day workers like Ingram and Hungerford seem to be concentrating on the systematic development of specific responses. This appears to be a radical switch from stimuli to response.[3]

Today's advocates of movement training return to physiological education as basic. To these contemporary theorists it appears that neither social competence nor vocational preparation nor emotional stability nor intelligent participation in activities is possible if basic modalities are not organized first. However, they are far from being a naive echo of the early advocates of sense training. They have developed their theories in a world that has experienced a tremendous growth in the understanding of physiology, child development, perception, learning, and education. They have developed their theories among professionals who now distinguish many subtypes among those who were earlier designated as mentally retarded. They are aware of "hyperactive children," "withdrawn children," "brain-damaged children," "subtrainable, trainable, and educable children," "autistic children," "perceptually handicapped children," "children with learning disabilities," and so on.

A brief review of the work of Kephart, Delacato, Getman, Frostig, and Barsch will serve to demonstrate their similarities and differences and their kinship with those described earlier.

None of these writers would disagree with the need for social competence, vocational training, emotional health, and academic training. They all seem to agree, however, that certain preparation is essential before any of these areas can be dealt with.

Kephart points out that when a child enters school we assume that a certain amount of learning has already taken place. He refers to the informal curriculum of the home preschool years that is supposed to assure the development of readiness skills. But a child who is not "intact," says Kephart, is not sufficiently trained in this informal atmosphere. A child who is not intact organically or emotionally learns in a different manner and needs more time to learn.[9]

Kephart maintains that motoric skills form the basis for all future learning. All movement is at first undifferentiated. Through experience, individual parts of the body are first differentiated and then integrated in a cephalo-caudal and in a proximodistal sequence. If one part is differentiated in isolation (out of sequence) it never becomes fully incorporated in total body movement and is referred to as a "splinter skill." The *way* in which a child develops is more important to Kephart than the point at which he has arrived.

Once the motor system is functioning efficiently, perceptual information can be processed and matched with motor patterns. Kephart offers motoric and visual-motor training as fundamental to future learning.

Of these two developmental ingredients Delacato stresses the motor and Getman stresses the visual.

It is Delacato's theory that all problems of communication originate in inadequate neurological organization and the failure of the human organism to develop unilaterality. He considers unilaterality to be "that dynamic aspect of neurological organization which distinguishes man from lower animals."[10] Delacato is concerned with the ontogenetic recapitulation of phylogenetic development. The human organism, he says, represents the highest neurological development yet achieved. Man has added a final state of laterality. "The basic difference between man and the animal world is that man has achieved cortical dominance wherein one side of the cortex controls the skills in which man outdistances lower forms of animals."

When a child's symbolic functioning is limited, Delacato works to establish neurological unity. He "set[s] the neurological train reaction in order" by making the entire child one-sided and minimizing the role of the nondominant hemisphere. Basic to such serialization is proper posturalization. Training for the child involves passive manipulation in reflex movement patterns, patterning of sleep position, crawling, training for eye dominance, handedness, and footedness. The curriculum calls for the elimination of all tonal experience (there is no music, and reading is conducted in a whisper to eliminate the role of the nondominant hemisphere which Delacato believes controls all tonal experience). It also calls for dietary restrictions to limit fluid intake (an excess of spinal fluid cuts down oxygen supply to the cortex), and sometimes breathing into a plastic bag for short periods to raise the level of carbon dioxide in the blood (to force the cortex to make better use of available oxygen), and other techniques generally considered to be unorthodox. The Delacato approach has been the focus of sharp criticism and much diversity of opinion.

G. N. Getman, an optometrist by training, boldly claims that vision is intelligence. "Intelligence," he says, "is the ability to make a judgment, decision, or action best suited to the problem of the movement, based upon the total knowledge gained from one's experience."[11] He aims to integrate biological and cultural intelligence by supplying a meaningful experiental background. Getman's sequence demands training in general motor patterns, the development of special movement patterns leading to hand-eye coordination, the development of eye movement patterns which substitute for and thus reduce exploratory movement, communication patterns which also replace action, and visual patterns to supply skill in comparison, visual memory, and visual projection. This sequence leads to the final stage, the development of visual perceptual organization. ". . . [I]f development and experience have followed the usual and expected course through the first ten years, a child learns to use vision as the primary process to guide his own actions." Vision is now ready to play a basic role in concept formation. For Getman, the primary needs of our culture are visual and auditory, with greater stress on the former. Kinesthetic development is recognized as a foundation for the other modalities.

Marianne Frostig's training program emphasizes the area of visual perception.[12] Like Getman, she considers vision to be the most important modality. Maximal visual development takes place during the years from three-and-one-half to seven-and-one-half. If there is a lag in this development, all other functioning is affected. Frostig finds a correlation between scores achieved on her test of visual perception and both academic achievement and personal adjustment. Visual perception, says Frostig, is the process by which stimuli are recognized, interpreted, and identified through correlation with past experiences. Although there are two major senses, hearing and vision, vision is the most important and is basic to academic survival.

Frostig's test, and the training based on the test results, establishes five areas that develop independently and may be disturbed independently and in varying degrees. Visual perception is a compilation of visual-motor coordination, figure-ground discrimination, perceptual constancy, awareness of position in space and of spatial relationships.

Frostig's development sequence is from the sensory-motor development of the first two years to the emphasis on speech development that takes place up to the age of four, to the visual perceptual development from three-and-one half to seven-and-one-half, and to the development of higher cognitive processes that starts at seven, eight, or older.

The most highly organized approach to movement training is presented in Barsch's Movigenic Theory which studies the origin and development of movement patterns. Barsch speaks of physical, psychological, and physiological movement and the need to coordinate all three. He explains deviations as follows:

> The distortions, deviations, warps, confusions, and maladjustments of the individual become explainable in terms of movement failures. Some movement organization required for successful adaptation was not present and the resultant warp or confusion stems from the inability of the organism to efficiently resolve the task.[13]

Barsch says that a child must learn how to use the processing modalities in a meaningful way in order to function in his space world. The child must learn to translate the energies impinging on him, i.e. the light, the sound, the pressure that surrounds him, into meaningful patterns and experiences. When the movement around the child becomes meaningful to him then he himself will be able to move in a meaningful way that reflects what is happening in his environment.

The primary movement task involves movement through space. To master gravitational pull and to propel himself through space, the child must discover the dimensions of space and find their counterparts within himself. He must build movements in terms of up and down, side to side, forward and back.

As this organization takes place, the child is also building an ever-widening world for himself. The boundaries of this world are moving farther and farther away from himself. Pure sensation is becoming perception and cognition, and soon he will be able to communicate with symbols, concepts, and generalizations. But, Barsch tells us, none of this can occur without movement.

The individual is able to process information through six modalities: vision, audition, kinesthesia, tactuality, and the olfactory and gustatory senses. Four of these (vision, audition, kinesthesia, and tactuality) are basic to survival in our culture. Each individual uses these avenues with different emphasis, depending on the emphasis of his experience. A child can then be described as functioning through a modality hierarchy designated as VAKT, KATV, ATKV, and so on. In a very concise way this presents the strongest and weakest modalities available to the individual.

When we find that a child is having difficulty in school, it should be possible to examine his present functioning level, break it down into visual, auditory, kinesthetic, and tactual abilities, explore his orientation in space and a number of other components that Barsch has defined, and discover that at some time in this child's development basic processes failed to be organized.

An overview of these two groups of educators demonstrates that despite the span of more than a century and despite historic changes, there remains some commonality of approach to the human organism. The common link is agreement concerning modality function. Emphasis may differ, but all try, in one way or another, to explore the functioning of the sense modalities and to find ways to strengthen them. The modalities are seen as learning vehicles.

Many new educational approaches have been incorporated into our schools. Many have been dramatically successful. Within all of these successes, however, there still remain the few failures, the children who do not learn through old methods or new. There is every reason to believe that more intensive study of the area of modality function would be in keeping with the needs of today's educational philosophy and practice. Perhaps this is the key to future learning success for the few who still need our help.

REFERENCES

1. Boyd, William: *From Locke to Montessorri.* New York, Henry Holt, 1914.
2. Itard, Jean Marc: *The Wild Boy of Aveyron.* New York, Appleton-Century-Crofts, 1962.
3. Rothstein, Jerome H.: *Mental Retardation.* New York, Holt, Rinehart, and Winston, 1964.

4. Seguin, Edward: *Idiocy and Its Treatment by the Physiological Method.* New York, William Wood, 1866.

5. Standing, E. M.: *Maria Montessori: Her Life and Work.* New York, New Am. Lib., 1957.

6. Gesell, Arnold: *The Retarded Child: How to Help Him.* Bloomington, Public School, 1925.

7. Kirk, Samuel A.: *Educating Exceptional Children.* Boston, Houghton Mifflin, 1962.

8. Kirk, Samuel A., and Johnson, Orville G.: *Educating the Retarded Child.* Boston, Houghton Mifflin, 1951.

9. Kephart, Newell C.: *The Slow Learner in the Classroom.* Columbus, C. E. Merrill, 1960.

10. Delacato, C. H.: *The Treatment and Prevention of Reading Problems.* Springfield, Thomas, 1959.

11. Getman, G. N.: *How to Develop Your Child's Intelligence.* Luverne, 1957.

12. Frostig, Marianne, and Horne, David: *The Frostig Program for the Development of Visual Perception.* Chicago, Follett, 1964.

13. Barsch, Ray H.: Project M.O.V.E. as a Model for Rehabilitation Theory. From a summary based on a paper presented at the A.P.A. Convention, Philadelphia, 1963.

SECTION D

VISUAL PERCEPTUAL DISABILITIES

Chapter 9

VISUAL FUNCTION IN LEARNING DISABILITIES

NATHAN FLAX

A SURVEY OF THE LITERATURE relating visual function with learning disability, particularly to reading disability, is conspicuous for its lack of clear-cut relationships. This should not be surprising in view of the complexity of both visual function and the learning process. The problems of establishing adequately controlled research to ascertain the part played by visual function in learning disability are enormous. Nonetheless, it would seem logical that there are positive relationships between visual factors and learning disabilities since vision plays such an enormous role in the acquisition of information in the school surroundings. This paper will endeavor to explain visual function in order that some relationships between vision and learning disability may be made apparent.

Visual acuity and others of the more obvious visual functions do not correlate to learning ability. It is possible to be successful at reading with significantly poorer eyesight than 20/20. Refractive measurements also do not correlate particularly with scholastic success. There are certain types of refractive errors which seem to make it difficult for some people to read efficiently, but it is not possible to relate the magnitude of the impact on learning with the magnitude of the refractive error itself. In some instances relatively small refractive errors can seriously impair scholastic efficiency, while in other instances rather large refractive errors have little or no impact on scholastic performance. It requires a full clinical evaluation to determine what influence

Reprinted from the *Journal of Learning Disabilities*, Vol. 1 (1968), pp. 552-556. By permission of the author and the publisher.

a refractive error might have on a particular individual's functioning. The problem is further complicated because some refractive errors may actually represent adaptive responses which permit better scholastic performance. For this reason, group statistics can be expected to produce the equivocal results that have been demonstrated.

The term learning disability itself leads to confusion since it is so broad and encompasses so many different types of problems. In order to assess the role of visual function it becomes necessary to define more closely what is meant by learning disability, since different types of academic demands require different types of visual function. For instance, the visual requirements for learning to read in the lowest grades are quite different from the visual requirements necessary for lengthy reading with good comprehension in order to acquire information in the upper grades. The visual factors inherent in making the visual-verbal matchings necessary for word recognition are quite different from the visual factors necessary to utilize reading as a tool for learning. The dyslexic individual generally presents quite different visual measures than the individual who can read but who is inefficient at reading. It becomes necessary to differentiate between those visual factors which serve to interfere with the efficiency of the reading process and those visual factors which prevent acquisition of rudimentary word recognition skills.

MEANINGFUL READING

Sustained, meaningful reading is dependent upon the ability to maintain an easy flow of information from the printed page. Vision serves as a link in the transmission of data from the author's words to the reader. Any visual deficiency that would interfere with this free flow of information would tend to impair reading efficiency. Binocular fusion problems would be in this category. An individual who cannot maintain proper simultaneous use of both eyes may suffer from fatigue, discomfort, or loss of comprehension. Generally, this type of visual deficiency will not cause total failure at reading but will render reading less efficient. Further, it must be realized that the visual system is capable of adaptation within itself in order to permit better function at specific tasks. This factor makes it quite difficult to investigate the role of visual funtcion in reading on a simple correlational basis. In correlational studies it is generally assumed that an individual with complete binocular function rates higher in visual efficiency than an individual with partial binocular function, and that an individual with partial binocular function rates higher than an individual with no binocular function. In order words, the assumption is made that the requirements for successful reading covary with the clinical visual measurements. This is not necessarily so, since it becomes possible for an individual to read successfully on a one eye basis. An individual with a mild instability in his ability to utilize both eyes simultaneously may in fact be more handicapped at reading than an individual with an actual turned or crossed eye. From the point of view of clinical measurement, there is no question but that partial ability to use both eyes would be considered better visual function than an inability to ever use both eyes together. Yet, when the demands of reading are considered, it may actually be advantageous to totally shut off one eye rather than to struggle to maintain two-eyed vision inefficiently. In some cases binocular vision may worsen as school success goes up. This factor alone contributes to a good deal of the confusion in the literature.

INTERFERENCE OF VISUAL FUNCTION

One other aspect of visual function that frequently interferes with sustained reading is accommodation or focus ability. While most young people can adjust their eyes to see clearly at all distances, this adjustment, or accommodation, is not always done with proper facility. When there is difficulty in maintaining the proper focal adjustment, efficiency at reading, in terms of lowered comprehension, may be demonstrated long before there is actual blurring of print. In some children relatively minor accommodative problems are sufficient to produce discomfort and avoidance of reading.

Certain refractive errors—particularly hyperopia, differences in refractive measurements between the two eyes, and certain types of astigmatism—sometimes contribute to reading deficiency, but this can only be ascertained on the basis of an individual evaluation since the impact of these conditions varies considerably as a function of the individual's ability to compensate for them. These measurements do not lend themselves satisfactorily to group investigations.

Inability to control eye movement accurately is another factor which often contributes to inefficiency at reading. Faulty eye movement control often leads to careless errors, such as loss of place, substitutions, omissions, and, in general, reduces speed in comprehension.

Each of the individual factors mentioned thus far contributes to reading inefficiency by interfering with the ability to read accurately and comfortably. However, deficiencies in these visual skills cannot be responsible for a total inability to learn to read at all. The visual conditions which have been discussed thus far do not correlate highly with dyslexia (when dyslexia is defined as a total inability to read). This is not surprising since the dyslexic individual shows interference in a totally different aspect of visual function. The dyslexic cannot master basic word recognition skills and has not progressed to that point in reading where mild inefficiencies might be noticed.

VISION AND VISUAL PERCEPTION

In order to understand the contribution of visual function to the problem of dyslexia it is necessary to understand the development of vision and visual perception. Children who present hard core reading disability and who cannot learn to read at all show an inability to handle form and direction concepts on a visual basis and, in particular, show poor ability to integrate visual and auditory information. They are often described as showing a lag in visual perception.

Visual perception involves both innate and acquired skills. There are certain aspects of vision that are present and functioning on a reflex level right at birth. Proper development of vision requires interaction between growth and environmental factors. At birth, the newborn is capable of aiming his eyes toward bright light. These eye movements are not voluntary although the muscle systems that are activated are the very same muscle systems that must be used later in life to control voluntary eye movements. The stimulus to early eye aiming is brightness of illumination and certain physical characteristics of the stimulus rather than intellectual content of that which is being viewed. Reflex associations between audition and sight are also present at birth. The neonate will aim his eyes toward a loud noise. There are also reflex postural reflexes present which involve coordination between eye and body position. The fact that the infant, on a reflex basis, centers his attention auditorily, visually, and posturally toward the same point in space provides the basis for development of intersensory equivalence. This is a vital step in the development of perceptual abilities. Rather than random opportunity for intersensory exploration, there is a forced simultaneous investigation of the external environment utilizing more than one sense modality at the same time. This provides the opportunity for development of intersensory matchings which are so vital for later perceptual success.

Between infancy and school age the child has to develop ability to encode from one sense modality to another so that one sense modality can ultimately substitute for another. This is the basis for verbal and visual communication whereby abstractions and symbols can stand for objects and movements. Ultimately, if all proceeds well, it becomes possible to acquire the same information by looking at an object that would ordinarily be derived by touch, taste, or movement. At the outset, multisensory exploration is brought about via reflex associations between sensory motor systems. With maturation and development there must be an acquisition of intersensory equivalence, as well as the ability to gradually separate one sense modality from the other so as to avoid the need for redundancy in exploration. Many children in the dyslexic category show a deficiency in one or the other phases of this aspect of development. They either show poor sensory integration or they show a persistent need for multisensory inputs. Either problem would impair visual perception abilities, although not in exactly the same way.

It must be kept in mind that standard pedagogical programs assume the ability to utilize visual function (as well as auditory function) independent of the opportunity for immediate tactile and movement support. (Public schools teach through the ears and eyes primarily, thus ignoring touch and movement.) The standard teaching program also assumes that visual attention can be centered toward that which is deemed culturally important even though the primitive reflex aiming mechanisms for vision are responsive primarily to the physical intensity of the stimulation. There must be a gradual development of ability to override the early reflex associations and the early reflex multisensory attention in favor of a more selective attention on the basis of volitional or voluntary control and, along with this, the ability to utilize one sense in place of another.

In the normal course of development of visual perception there are a number of stages wherein the hierarchal relationship between the different sensory-motor modes changes. The role of vision should become increasingly dominant as normal development proceeds. Hopefully, at the time that formal instruction is begun in reading and writing, the child should be able to function so that shape, form, and direction constancy can be obtained via input eye signals without the need for movement and tactile support. This aspect of visual function is frequently defective in the dyslexic child. Failure of adequate visual perception and visuo-motor development is characteristic of the dyslexic.

The role of visual function in learning disability may run the gamut from interferences in the more mechanical aspects of vision (such as binocular fusion, accommodation, and eye aiming), which will limit efficiency at the reading activity, to a failure of development of adequate visual perception abilities which will make it impossible to develop fundamental word recognition skills. Adequate investigation of visual function to insure optimum opportunity for learning must involve standard eye examination procedures for ocular health, refractive error, and acuity, along with functional investigation into binocular coordination, accommodative or focus ability, and eye movement skills. The investigation must also involve probing into intersensory development with particular emphasis upon the ability to integrate sensory-motor data and posture information with incoming visual data. This ability is needed to permit adequate matching of visual configuration with language constructs. Utilization of this approach discloses meaningful relationships between visual function and learning disability.

REFERENCES

1. Bing, Lois B.: A critical analysis of the literature on certain visual functions which seem to be related to reading achievement. *J Am Optom Assoc*, 22:454-63, 1951.
2. Birch, Herbert G., and Belmont, Lillian: Auditory visual integration in normal and retarded readers. *Am J Orthopsychiatry*, 34:852-861, October 1964.
3. Eames, Thomas H.: Visual handicaps to reading. *J Educ*, 141:1-35, 1959.
4. Flax, Nathan: Visual factors which affect reading achievement. *Optom Weekly*, 58 (No. 29):19-25, July 20, 1967.
5. Flax, Nathan: The development of vision and visual perception: implications in learning disability. Proceedings of 1967 International Convocation on Children and Young Adults With Learning Disabilities, Home for Crippled Children, Pittsburgh, pp. 130-134.
6. Flax, Nathan: Visual Function in Dyslexia. *Am J Optom.* In press.
7. Huelsman, Charles B. Jr.: Some recent research in visual problems in reading. *Am J Optom*, 35:559-64, 1958.
8. Spache, George D.: Children's vision and their reading success. *J California Optom Assoc*, 29, No. 5, August-September 1961.

Chapter 10

VISUAL PERCEPTION AND READING

IRVING L. SHAPIRO

W E ARE LIVING in the jet age—the atomic age. This is a period of civilization characterized by tremendous, limitless power. There are exploding needs for human resources, yet these are not being developed effectively. The mere fact that a child has good health, possesses average intellectual ability, and is exposed to the growing cultural demands of civilization does not mean that he is prepared to understand or cope with this culture.

One may wonder how the above is related to vision, visual perception and testing, and to reading; I believe, very significantly.

Many years ago, when optometry first came into existence, our concern was with sharpness and distance acuity. Through the years, our concern for effective control of the eyes and the visual focus at near-point reading distance became more manifest. There were too many conditions for which the 20/20 distance chart did not provide. Thinking of vision in terms of focusing of the eyes alone left too many problems unsolved.

There are five aspects of vision with which we are concerned:

1. Health of the eyes.
2. Acuity of sight; near and far distances.
3 Control of the eyes; their ability to work together as a team.
4. Skillful use of the eyes; the ability to follow a moving object, and to go from point-to-point accurately; and, among other skills, speed and span of recognition.

Reprinted from the *Academic Therapy Quarterly*, Vol. 2 (1967), pp. 227-235. By permission of the author and publisher.

5. Visual perception ability to make accurate judgments as to size, spacial relations, form configuration, and visualization.

It is readily discernible from these five points that items 3, 4, and 5 are manifestations of vision which are highly adaptable and trainable. They form an important basis for reading readiness. Any deterioration or enhancement in their performance is directly related to reading ability. In recent years, the research of the Optometric Extension Foundation and the work of the Gesell Institute of Child Development have brought us a realization of the need to integrate our thinking in terms of a number of controls.[1] The eye sees; this is sight. But the mind interprets; this is vision. There are four basic controls associated with an active mind that produce vision as we think of it now.

These circles can help us illustrate this concept.

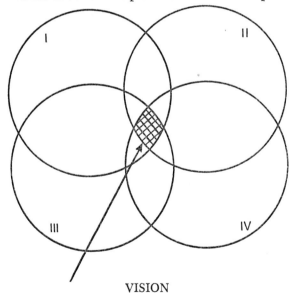

VISION

I. Centering
   Centering eyes on an object (aligning each eye).
II. Focusing
   Refining and discrimination.
III. Locomotion
   Body control in relation to gravity.
IV. Language
   Speech and auditory.

VISION

Circle I. Centering refers to the ability of the individual to first align his eyes upon a given object in space and center the regard of both eyes on the object as it moves or as he moves his eyes from near to far or from side to side. This calls for delicate control and organization.

Circle II. Focusing indicates the ability of the individual to refine and discriminate detail and texture with each eye and then both eyes at all distances.

Circle III. Locomotion indicates the need of the individual to have effective body movement patterns and to move arms, legs, and the complete body effectively in space.

Circle IV. Language indicates the need of the individual to have effective language control and usage; this includes the integration of vocabulary, language, and hearing.

Each of these areas deals with effective movement and control. It is the delicate integration of all these skills and abilities related to the mental process that produces vision. Lacking good and effective movements, controls, and effective expressions in all these areas means poor vision.

Thinking of vision in these broader terms, what is the optometrist concened with in observing? What type of tests would he use? What type of training or correction would he employ?

There are six general areas of movement related to vision with which the vision specialist is greatly concerned. These help determine how capable a child is in visual perception and his readiness for education and reading. These areas are

1. General Movement Pattern
2. Specific Movement Pattern
3. Eye Movement Pattern
4. Vision-Language Area
5. Visualization
6. Visual Perception Organization

General Movement Pattern

The general movement pattern employs the long muscles of the body. The child should be able to move his body freely in good coordination and control in all directions. What I speak of here is the ability of the child to balance himself effectively against gravity. This may be illustrated, for example, by having a child use a balance board, or by having him walk a 2 × 4 inch beam.

Specific Movement Patterns

By specific movement patterns, I refer to the hand and eye control. How well can the child manipulate and contact objects in space? Studies have shown that most of the progress of civilization has been achieved through man's effective integration of mind, eye, and hand.

> Full performance and comprehension of "the world" cannot come until the eyes and hands are used in unified combination to probe and minutely explore "the world." A child must have the opportunities to "feel what things see like—and to see what things feel like."[2]

In this respect, an important series of tests and training devices in eye-hand manipulation and perception is the perceptual copy forms used in the Winter Haven, Florida, Visual Perception and Development Program.[6] The correlation of effective scholastic ability and successful performance on these devices is very high. An excellent handbook has been written on this subject.[8]

Other training aids in this area are cut-outs, jigsaw puzzles, tinker toys, and pegboards.

Eye Movement Patterns

The control of eye movements is an essential ability if visual inspections are to be effective and efficient. The child who lacks eye movement controls cannot "see at a glance," and must spend additional time and energy in making visual discriminations. As a result, ocular motilities are an absolute essential to visual developments and visual perception will be inadequate or incomplete if eye movements are jerky and restricted.

Statistical studies made by Lyons and Lyons on eye movements show significant relationships as related to school achievement tests.[3-5]

Dorothy Simpson, in her doctoral thesis at Purdue University, titled *Perceptual Readiness and Beginning Reading*, showed how training in eye movements as part of a schoolroom program helped one group of children gain from nine to thirteen academic months in three calendar months.

There have been hundreds of studies made on the relationships of vision and school achievement, but most of these studies are based on distance acuity. However, there is no correlation between distance acuity and ability to do close work. The more recent studies based on eye movement are much more productive in showing these correlations to school achievement.

Naturally, when a professional visual analysis is made, one of the first things to look for is smooth ability to follow a moving object, and to go from object to object easily. An easy test which can be made by teachers is the push-up. As a pencil is drawn up to the child's eyes, if he sees double or one eye turns out at a distance of four inches or beyond from the bridge of his nose, trouble is indicated.

Following are some exercises to develop motility:

1. A ball is suspended from a string, with the string attached to the ceiling. The child is instructed to keep his eye on the ball as it rotates.

2. The teacher picks up one object at a time from a variety of objects in his lap. They are shown to the child at each side, to the left or to the right. The teacher uses his right hand and his left.

3. Utilizing the blackboard, we develop effective hand and eye coordination and effective body and eye movement patterns. Here, directional recognition, a basis for perception, has a chance to develop.

One should attempt to draw circles with both hands at the same time in these indicated directions as he observes the X in the center.

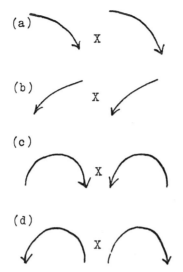

One should also attempt to draw straight lines with both hands at the same time, to and away from the central X, as indicated, working from opposite sides at the same time.

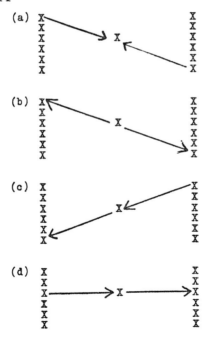

Blackboard work of this nature has helped children develop better handwriting, better coordination, and better visualization and perception.

While I have indicated these as tests, training may readily be instituted by repetition in the proper manner with guidance in weak areas.

Vision-Language Arts

I am interested in the vision-language relationship that comes out of seeing and listening, visualizing and saying, in order to extend skill in communication.

It is important that we recognize the close relationship between vision and language so they may provide guidance procedures that assist their child to develop skill in his communications with others. These guidance procedures must include activities that put emphasis upon audition and articulation as they are related to visual clues.

Likenesses and differences exist in sounds that can be heard, just as they exist in shapes that can be seen. The child who lacks skill in the auditory perception of sounds will have trouble in remembering what he has heard. These children often fail to retain stories read to them because their auditory perception of the story will be incomplete or inaccurate. They confuse words that sound alike, and they forget when sent on errands. These children are accused too frequently of not paying attention. This is often the same child who has difficulty later in recalling the words in reading because of forgetting the word told him by the teacher, or because he confuses it with a word of similar sound and shape. The visualization that should be brought to the child's mind by the word may be confused. These children usually have difficulty in utilizing phonetics as a method of attack on new words.[2]

Vocabulary plays an important role in a child's ability to visualize. A child of limited vocabulary has a limited visual memory.

Teachers are familiar with numerous methods of training children in language development, such as pictures and stories, and descriptive and action games using verbs, adjectives, adverbs, and prepositions. These are all helpful in developing a child's ability in vision-language organization. The following are a few of the training devices in this area:

1. The teacher taps on a table, then has the child recount the number of taps. The beat should be varied, tapping loudly and softly, quickly, then in irregular rhythm.

2. The teacher has the child identify noises and sounds and locate where or from whom they came. This gives him a chance to identify his auditory judgment against his visual impression.

3. The teacher first expresses digits in a monotone. The student either repeats them or writes them down.

Visualization Ability

The orderly development of the sequences previously described brings the child to the level where his vision alone can help provide him with much informaiton in the world about him. It should not be necessary now for him to touch and feel every familiar object he sees.

In this respect, the child must have good skills in the following:

1. Visual comparison.
2. Visual memory.
3. Visual projection.

When the child reads, he is confronted with visual cues only. He cannot depend on his hands to assist him. Skills must be acquired in the activities which will eventually assist him to see and recognize the differences and similarities between B and D, b and d, H and N, p and q, and many other letter forms. Inadequacies in this area of vision perception skills permit reversals in spelling and writing which plague so many primary-grade children.

Practice and training in the visualization skills can be given. Here are a few in each of the areas mentioned:

Visual Comparison Training

1. Have the child put together simple jigsaw puzzles.

2. Have the child match and compare objects in a room, such as furniture or books. Have him describe the likenesses and differences.

3. Have the child keep his eyes closed as he describes an object which you hand to him.

4. Write spelling words on a chalkboard. Have the child run his fingers over the letters of the word several times. Then have him step back beyond arm's reach and trace the letters in the air several times. Have him go back to the blackboard and write the letters again.

Visual Memory Training

1. Place several toys on a table, have the child look at the objects for several seconds. Then have the child look away and name the objects.

2. Expose a picture out of a catalogue or magazine, and have the child look at the picture. Cover it, then have him recall as many things as he remembers seeing.

3. Expose a simple pattern for a few seconds. Remove it and have the child draw it from memory.

Visual Projection

This is actually the use of visual comparison and visual memory for imaginative thinking. The child's skill in combining these two into speech and later into drawing and writing is the ultimate in use of visualization. This is a medium whereby the child becomes a participant instead of an observer.

1. Describe something and have the child name it from your description.

2. Have the child tell you, in detail, how to get from his house to someone else's home.

3. Have the child tell about places that are *not* familiar everyday trips, such as places visited on a vacation trip, what was done there, who was visited, and some of the details he saw there.

Visual Perception Organization

Organization of visual perception is a significant stage in the development of a total child. It is an exceedingly important stage in the development of intellectual capabilities. It is the end result of sequences and interweaving relationships that come out of the processes just described.

Perceptual organization furnishes the body mechanisms, the ability for the interpretation, understanding, and concepts of our world and its contents. The simplest examples of this ability are in the eye-hand interchange.

Here, we humans can feel an object, and when perceptual development has progressed as it should, we can describe the appearance of the object without looking at it. The most complex example is the visual interpretation of symbols, such as words, formuli, and maps, into speech or action of hands. Visual perception is the most significant of all our interpretative skills because vision as a distance receptor can help us to understand our world more completely than any other sensory mechanism.[2]

Finally, I believe that teachers are in the best position to recognize problems of vision requiring visual analysis. I wish to list the Teachers' Guide to Vision Problems, with check list.[9] This test can be obtained by writing the American Optometric Association, 7000 Chippewa Street, St. Louis, Missouri 63119.

TEACHER'S GUIDE TO VISION PROBLEMS
(With Check List)

To aid teachers in detecting the children who should be referred for complete visual analysis, the American Optometric Association Committee on Visual Problems in Schools has compiled a list of symptoms, a guide to vision problems. The committee recommends:

1. That all children in the lower third of the class, particularly those with ability to achieve above their percentile rating, be referred for complete visual analysis.

2. That every child in the class who, even though achieving, is not working up to within reasonable limits of his own capacity be referred for a complete visual analysis.

Following are other symptoms which may indicate a visual problem, regardless of results in any screening test. (The starred items were found to be particularly significant in a recent study.)

Observed in Reading

Dislike for reading and reading subjects
Skipping or rereading lines
*Losing place while reading
Slow reading or word calling
Desire to use finger or marker as pointer while reading

*Avoiding close work
*Poor sitting posture and position while reading
Vocalizing during silent reading, noticed by watching lips or throat
Reversals persisting in grade two or beyond
Inability to remember what has been read
Complaint of letters and lines "running together" or of words "jumping"
*Holding reading closer than normal
*Frowning, excessive blinking, scowling, or other facial distortions while reading
*Excessive head movements while reading
Poor perceptual ability, such as confusing o and a; n and m.

Other Manifestations

Restlessness, nervousness, irritability, or other unaccounted for behavior
Writing with face too close to work
Fatigue or listlessness after close work
Inattentiveness, temper tantrums, or frequent crying
Complaint of blur when looking up from close work
Seeing objects double
Headaches, dizziness, or nausea associated with the use of the eyes
*Body rigidity while looking at distant objects
Undue sensitivity to light
Crossed eyes—turning in or out
Red-rimmed, crusted, or swollen lids
Frequent sties
Watering or bloodshot eyes
Burning or itching of eyes or eyelids
*Tilting head to one side
*Tending to rub eyes
Closing or covering one eye.
Frequent tripping or stumbling.
Poor hand and eye coordination as manifested in poor baseball playing, batting and catching, or similar activities.
*Thrusting head forward.
*Tension during close work.
Only a complete case study will determine whether inadequate vision is a significant factor in nonachievement.

We professional people, whose responsibility it is to educate, guide, and care for children, are confronted with a tremendous challenge. We can help shape a generation of adults with great ability and power to create and achieve skills and goals which have been mankind's urge for centuries. A successful effort can result only in a better world for all to live in.

REFERENCES

1. Gesell, Arnold L., Ilg, Frances L., and Bullis, Glenna E.: *Vision, Its Development in Infant and Child.* New York. Paul B. Hoeber, 1949.
2. Getman, G. N.: *How to Develop Your Child's Intelligence.* Luverne, Minn., Self-published, 1960.
3. Lyons, C. V., and Lyons, E. B.: The powers of visual training as measured in factors of intelligence. *Am J Optometry,* December 1954.
4. ———— Further case studies measured in factors of intelligence. *Am J Optometry,* December 1956.
5. ———— The power of optometric visual training IV to build minds. *Am J Optometry,* June 1961.
6. *Perceptual Testing and Training Manual.* Winter Haven, Winter Haven Lions Club.
7. Skeffington, A. M.: *Texts on Functional Vision Care.* Duncan, Okla., Optom Ext Program, 1960.
8. Sutphin, Florence D.: *A Perceptual Testing and Training Handbook for First Grade Teachers.* Winter Haven, Winter Haven Lions Research Foundation 1964.
9. *Teacher's Guide to Vision Problems with Check List.* St. Louis, American Optometric Association.

SECTION E

AUDITORY-PERCEPTUAL AND LANGUAGE DISABILITIES

Chapter 11

PROGRAMING FOR AUDITORIALLY DISABLED CHILDREN

Francis X. Blair

In a previous paper[2] the term "aural deficiency" was proposed to refer to a group of diverse problems in which the auditory system is incapable of providing the child with acoustic information in a normal manner to the detriment of his speech, language, and in some cases, cognitive development. The auditory system is viewed as being composed of the neuroanatomical pathways extending from the end organ to the auditory cortex, and particularly Wernicke's area.[5] Disruptions in this system may result in a variety of auditory disorders, including reduced sensitivity to the sound spectrum, phonemic discrimination difficulties, disruptions of the temporal sequencing of speech messages, and imperfect comprehension of spoken language related to disturbances in the auditory association areas of the language dominant hemisphere.

NATURE OF AUDITORY DISABILITY

A schematized concept of the auditory receptive behavioral system is presented in Table 11-I. It indicates a hierarchy of auditory function which serves the development of the individual and his psychic adjustment in a variety of ways.

It is essential to acknowledge the possibility of a variety of aural disruptions occurring at different levels or stages along a continuum. In the first instance the individual must be auditorially sensitized to the raw sensory data of the environment.

Reprinted from *Exceptional Children*, Vol. 36 (1969), pp. 259-264. By permission of the author and publisher.

TABLE 11-I

DIMENSIONS OF AUDITORY RECEPTIVE BEHAVIOR

INPUT		
Sensory Contact	*Signal Acceptance*	*Symbol Association*
Sensitivity to relevant sound frequencies	Listening set (attention)	Sequential assimilation (temporal order memory)
Directional hearing	Figure-ground choice	Semantic recognition (long term memory)
	Acoustic analysis (discrimination)	

Fundamental needs of survival and adaptability as well as prelinguistic and precognitive stages of development are served. Basic environmental contact is made. Directionality is important to the extent that it contributes to these needs. At the level of signal acceptance the organism perceptually integrates auditory information in a meaningful or purposeful manner. At this level, the organism selectively tunes in to the environment, learns to identify and discriminate among the large array of data available to it, and attend to that which becomes subjectively relevant. Speech sounds, vocal utterances, and a variety of other environmental sounds having affective significance become a part of the ongoing input activity.

It is obvious that up to this point there is little essential difference between the auditory behavior of the human and that of the animal. The animal, for example, is responsive to certain affective stimuli and can even discriminate among acoustic patterns, including speech signals, to the extent that it is trained or that these data become relevant to its needs in other ways.

We have been concerned with what might be called presymbolic stages in audition. These are highly essential stages in normal human development; what transports the human beyond the animal is the cortical apparatus which permits the construction of cognition and symbolic language. This is fundamentally an auditory vocal language which eventually becomes the basis for written language.

The term aural deficiency as originally proposed was intended to connote a variety of disorders which are known by a myriad of labels: the deaf, hard of hearing, and those individuals having auditory perceptual handicaps, auditory agnosia, auditory imperception, and receptive aphasia, to specify a few. The present concern, however, is with those who are nondeaf, those who have an amount of residual hearing or even normal acuity but who, nontheless, cannot function effectively in the acoustic environment for various reasons. The concern expressed here is for the inadequate educational management of what may constitute a significant population of developmentally and academically deprived children.

Traditionally, professionals have been somewhat stimulus bound to diagnostic categories, possibly for valid reasons of administrative management. A more recent and encouraging trend in special education has been the emphasis on the identification of the behavioral dimensions of the disability or the analysis of basic learning processes in an individual, rather than the assumption of certain conditions based on a diagnostic label. Increased concern for children with special learning disabilities has helped to foster this philosophy of identifying the specific areas of the disability, i.e. auditory, visual, tactile; sensory, perceptual, or conceptual, which require remediation in order to permit the learner to realize his achievement potential.[8, 9]

In a real sense, then, when we concern ourselves with aural deficiency in the above context, we are properly referring to children having auditory learning disabilities, and it is suggested that this term be adopted in reference to these children.

Evidence derived from educational programs suggests that a significant percentage of children classified as deaf are not merely deaf but are displaying characteristics which require teaching insights and methods which extend beyond the traditional approaches.[1, 12, 13] Similarly, it is obvious that those sustaining lesser degrees of acoustic impairment are frequently multiply handicapped in the sense that the primary disability is compounded by disruptive events at the perceptual-sequential-associative levels of the auditory system. This is not to overlook the distinct likelihood of the additional occurrence of visual perceptual and motor integrative disabilities in the same children. Obviously, educational programing must recognize the existence of all process defects and their relationship to the total disruption of learning in an individual child. It is to the needs of these children that this article is primarily addressed.

NEED FOR EARLIER DETECTION

There would be some professional agreement that the condition of gross deafness is recognizable at a relatively early age although there would be somewhat less agreement regarding the management steps to be taken in infancy and very early childhood. The identification of auditory dysfunctions which are less than gross in the sheer acoustic sense is a great deal more problematical and is analogous in some respects to the detection at an early age of those children having borderline retardation or other conditions of partial disability. One reason for this appears to be the frequent lack of dramatic symptoms which serve to point up the child's need. Partial development of speech and language may occur, thereby inhibiting the arousal of anxiety in parents which often serves as the motivating device for them to seek professional assistance. Frequently, the consequence is that such children are carried along with an aura of optimism until nursery school or kindergarten age or later. The ever present hope of the child's outgrowing the difficulty frequently contributes to this procrastination.

The question must be asked, by what means can the partially auditorially disabled be discovered and, even more importantly, whose responsibility do they become? Again, to use the analogy of the marginally mentally retarded, this is often a function of appropriate evaluative instruments as well as the establishment of systematic case finding procedures. In the field of audiology the work of Downs and her colleagues[3] has been an important pioneering effort to establish a methodology for early detection of severe hearing impairment. The apparent small returns from such an undertaking should not vitiate the ultimate value of the procedure. As indicated above, the detection of those with lesser degrees of impairment or with more exotic types of auditory disorders presents significant problems, particularly with respect to proper evaluate procedures and behavioral response criteria. It seems possible that eventual refinements of the Downs approach may emerge for this purpose, but a large amount of research is necessary.

NEED FOR PRESCHOOL SERVICES AND PROGRAMS

The question of appropriately timed services for those having auditory learning disabilities is intimately related to the recognition of the need and, therefore, to early detection. If, as presently seems the case, those children with less obvious disorders are not identified until about the age of four years, there would appear to be compelling reasons to seriously explore some modes of attack on this problem.

Community education involving the public at large is an obvious first step. Related to this is the appropriate orientation of medical personnel concerning the significance of the early years in the development of communicative and cognitive abilities. The Head Start concept has served an important function in this regard but it needs to be extended to other disabilities.

Pediatric and otolaryngological professionals have played an important role in alerting parents and the community to the possible consequences of the recent rubella epidemic. As a result, it appears that a number of children so affected were identified at age two or three years.

The mechanics of complaint detection and referral remains a fundamental area of concern. If it requires a cyclical epidemic such as rubella to force a large effort toward early identification then we are in serious trouble. What seems to be necessary is the establishment of routine procedures for the screening of all newborn children. Admittedly we are without good screening techniques for the infant, but it is not likely that these will be developed outside the framework of a well organized effort.

The implementation of such a massive effort may seem unlikely within the framework of a nontotalitarian society but the recent growth of national concern for large segments of our population, including the deprived and the aged, suggests philosophical readiness for such a movement. What is necessary is money and manpower.

The author would like to propose the concept of child conservation centers. These would be medical-educational facilities strategically located to serve large population areas. Such centers would be funded by local, state, and federal governments and be partially self-supporting. They would provide a variety of diagnostic and remediation services, incorporating the coordinated skills of medicine, psychology, education, speech pathology and audiology, and social service. There should be particular concern with the educational aspects of such a concept because of the serious lack at the present time of preschool education, including proper counseling for parents.

From the educational point of view it is becoming increasingly obvious that the early discovery and diagnosis of learning disabilities in children must be less concerned with diagnostic classification and more concerned with the developmental and behavioral inadequacies of physical, mental, and social growth. The similarity, for example, of certain of the early characteristics of the culturally disadvantaged, the mildly retarded, the learning disabled, and the emotionally disturbed suggests that initial programs of habilitation need not be markedly different. They need to be developmentally oriented. This point of view does not deny the need for differential diagnosis as a means of specifying particular needs of the individual. This is especially true for the child with a significant auditory disorder for whom amplification may be critical, for example. But the primary function of the conservation center would be to provide services and programs for the young child, services and programs which are now inadequate, fragmented, or even lacking. This is not intended to be a criticism of the services provided for many years and still provided by hearing societies, speech and hearing clinics, and other agencies, but it appears that these groups are working too often in relative isolation. There is need to strive for more effective machinery which will link these community services to the educational system. In a sense, what is suggested here is a greater involvement of the educational system at the preschool level for all children but, in terms of our concern here, especially for the exceptional child.

NEED FOR SCHOOL PROGRAMS

With respect to the child with auditory learning disabilities, there is also a need for drastic action at the nursery and primary school levels. There are many instances of such a child reaching school age and being unable to find placement according to his needs. Such children, despite the fact that they are not deaf, are frequently placed in classes for the deaf. Other similar children are place in regular classrooms. It is surprising how little regard the typical educational system has shown toward the child with these kinds of disabilities. There may be legitimate reasons for this circumstance. It seems quite probable that those involved in education and rehabilitation have failed to adequately demonstrate the unique needs of the hard of hearing, the language disordered, and others falling generally into this classification. The professional literature has only recently carried any description of the special problems and requirements of these cases.[4, 6, 7, 10, 14]

The needs of such children who are placed in classes for the deaf are typically assumed to be consonant with those of the severely deaf child, and as a result, there frequently is an emphasis on oral education and a de-emphasis on aural habilitation. The needs of such children in the regular classroom are assumed by many to be minimal, and all of us probably share the blame for perpetuating the myth of preferential seating and token therapy as fulfilling the need for educational compensation. These malfeasances are so widely practiced as to have become established educational policies in most day and residential programs for the hearing impaired.

Probably the major reason for this circumstance is the scarcity of proper programing for children with auditory learning disabilities, i.e. the hard of hearing and those with auditory vocal language disorders (aphasia). Several types of facilities urgently needed are

1. *Transitional program* at the kindergarten and primary level for the marginal hearing disabilities cases. It is anticipated that

such programs would serve as a bridge between preschool educational programs and regular school programs. These units would be taught by regular primary teachers who have had special preservice or inservice orientation to the needs of the hearing disabled.

2. *Fulltime special classes* for the moderate to moderately severe hard of hearing and multiply handicapped hard of hearing child. Such classes should be taught by a teacher of children with auditory learning disabilities and should be established probably for grades one through three.

3. *Resource rooms* to meet the needs for many of the children described above who may be able to integrate into regular classrooms possibly by grade four. Such room might also serve the severely deaf who have been integrated into regular classes. These teachers would be trained in the area of auditory learning disabilities; some of them would be permanently stationed in particular schools and others would be itinerant.

4. *Regional educational centers* for all exceptional children including those with the different hearing disabilities. These centers would be particularly essential outside the larger metropolitan areas in situations where there is need for consolidation to serve large geographical units.

NEED FOR A TEACHER OF CHILDREN WITH AUDITORY LEARNING DISABILITIES

This concept is a derivative of the teacher of special learning disabilities, as previously defined. It is based on the notion that teacher preparation programs are currently failing to acknowledge the special characteristics of a population of children who have intellectual potential and the capacity for learning but who are not able to achieve at expectancy level. By implication, many of these children have neurological disorders as a basis for their atypical development, while others may have emotional disorders. Combinations of these conditions are also commonly found.

The teacher of these children should combine the best professional characteristics of the regular teacher, the teacher of the deaf, the teacher of special learning disabilities, and the speech and language therapist. This teacher concept extends beyond the idea of the hearing therapist or rehabilitative audiologist as proposed by O'Neill.[11] Such personnel are evidently not being trained at the moment. A rationale for such a teacher is implicit in the above discussion, and the following subjects are suggested as some of the significant elements of a good training curriculum: general child development; psychology of the exceptional child; pathology of auditory and visual perception; language development and applied linguistics; speech and language pathology; auditory training and hearing aids; speech reading methods; writing, spelling, and arithmetic disability; psychoeducational diagnostic techniques; methods of teaching academic subjects; student teaching with normal children; and student teaching with children having auditory learning disabilities. Obviously, at this point in time any curriculum is tentative and needs to be experimentally tested and evaluated.

NEED FOR PROFESSIONAL COORDINATION

Educational programming for any classification of exceptional children can develop and succeed only to the extent that the need for programs is demonstrated and that appropriately trained teaching personnel are available to implement services. Education cannot be expected to be effective without the proper use of related diagnostic specialists. For example, in the area of auditory learning disabilities, the potential contributions of the audiologist as well as the psychologist need to be realized.

The audiologist can best serve these children by continuing laboratory research and clinical study of the auditory behavior of both normal and exceptional children and, although he needs to be conversant with child psychology and the educative process, he should avoid the role of a psychodiagnostician, therapist, or teacher. The psychologist's value rests not only in his proficiency in the use of quantitative measuring instruments but, additionally, in his understanding of general behavior as it relates to the educative process.

The audiologist and the psychologist can contribute most effectively to the needs of these children by assisting teachers to better understand the functioning and dysfunctioning of the individual learner. Thus, these specialists can serve as significant catalysts in the achievement of pragmatic instructional methodology. It should be apparent, although it frequently is not, that the teacher is the expert in these matters as much as or more than the diagnostic specialists. Yet the teacher does need direct and meaningful assistance in translating clinical data into classroom procedures.

Each learning disabled child presents a different picture of educational requirements. We can no longer group children simply on the basis of categorical labels, although the labels retain some usefulness. Each child must be clinically analyzed and educationally approached as a unique learner, and special education can be successful only to the extent that each professional defines the limits of his own expertise and coordinates it with that of his professional allies.

REFERENCES

1. Blair, F. X.: An exploratory stury of unusual learning difficulties among deaf children in Wisconsin. Unpublished report, Milwaukee, University Wisconsin-Milwaukee, Department of Exceptional Education, 1964.
2. Blair, F. X.: Problems in the habilitation of aural deficiency. In Oyer, H. J. (Ed.): *Proceedings of Seminar on Aural Rehabilitation of the Acoustically Handicapped.* East Lansing, Michigan State University, 1966, pp. 1-23.
3. Downs, M. P., and Sterritt, G. M.: A guide to newborn and infant hearing screening programs. *Archives Otolaryngology,* 85:37-44, 1967.
4. Gaeth, J. H., and Lounsbury, E.: Hearing aids and children in elementary school. *J Speech & Hearing Disorders,* 31:283-287, 1966.
5. Geschwind, N.: Neurological foundations of language. In Myklebust, H. R. (Ed.): *Progress in Learning Disabilities.* New York, Grune and Stratton, 1968, Vol. 1.
6. Goetzinger, C. P.: Effects of small perceptive losses on language and on speech discrimination. *Volta Review,* 64:408-414, 1962.
7. Goetzinger, C. P., Harrison, C., and Baer, C. J.: Small perceptive hearing loss: Its effect in school-age children. *Volta Review,* 66:124-131, 1964.
8. Johnson, D., and Myklebust, H.: *Learning Disabilities: Educational Principles and Practices.* New York, Grune and Stratton, 1967.
9. Kirk, S. A., and Bateman, B.: Diagnosis and remediation of learning disabilities. *Excep Children,* 29:73-78, 1962.

10. Kodman, F., Jr.: Educational status of hard of hearing children in the classroom. *J Speech Hearing Disorders,* 28:297-299, 1963.
11. O'Neill, J. J.: Curricular models for aural rehabilitation training. In Oyer, H. J. (Ed.): *Proceedings of Seminar on Aural Rehabilitation of the Acoustically Handicapped.* East Lansing, Michigan State University, 1966, pp. 103-118.
12. Vernon, M.: The brain injured (neurologically impaired) child: A discussion of the significance of the problem, its symptoms and causes in deaf children. *Am Annals Deaf, 106:*239-250, 1961.
13. Vernon, M.: Characteristics associated with post-rubella deaf children. *Volta Review, 69:*176-185, 1967.
14. Watson, T. J.: The use of hearing aids by hearing impaired pupils in ordinary schools. *Volta Review, 66:*741-744, 1964.

Chapter 12

SELECTED METHODS OF INSTRUCTION FOR CHILDREN WITH COMMUNICATION DISORDERS

Edward G. Scagliotta

T HE AVENUES TO LEARNING are many. For those who possess normal intellect and coordinated physical development and whose senses are all functioning normally, sensory and motor endeavors of all varieties are open to experimentation. Acquired knowledge is basically the product of the perceptual motor concept in one or more of the areas of learning. If any of these senses or motor responses are denied, it becomes necessary for the individual to compensate by opening new avenues for learning. Accentuation of the unimpaired areas must be developed if the learning is to be accomplished.

In order for the perceptual process to function properly, each area must operate in correlation with all the others. Each area is influenced by what transpires in the one area. Thus, the total activity becomes an integrated process, although a specific area is to be trained. For the purpose of terminology let us call this process "simultaneous sensory motor training."

This term implies that sensory activities and motor activities are inseparable. What takes place in one area affects all others. If we parallel our thinking with that of a closed electrical circuit, our premise gains credence, and consideration of perception and muscular activities as separate entities is no longer possible.

Separating a child's task into its perceptual and motor parts is an analysis that no teacher should undertake. Having accepted the child as a whole organism functioning as a whole, the experienced and enlightened teacher is cognizant of the importance

Reprinted from *Education and Training Of The Mentally Retarded*, Vol. 2 (1967), pp. 164-176. By permission of the author and publisher.

and advantages of simultaneous sensory motor training. The end product of the teacher's endeavor becomes the sole criterion for judgment and evaluation of the child's mastery of the sensory motor process.

In training the child in the skills of communication, the utilization of the simultaneous sensory motor training concept brings into play as many of the sensory areas as possible, as well as the appropriate motor responses of the area so stimulated. In this way, the child is able to communicate with his environment by a number of means and is not limited by the mode of reception or expression. It is through compensation and the proper channeling of input that output becomes a success experience for the child.

PICTURE-WORD CARDS, ACTION FORM

The purposes of the action picture-word cards are to coordinate visual-auditory-kinesthetic and motor systems as a foundation for symbolic interpretation, to develop the comprehension of visual word configuration, to develop perception of lip and tongue movements, to develop conceptualization of concrete commands, and to reduce concomitant emotional overlay by providing success experiences.

For the child who has been diagnosed as having dysacousis, apraxia, and dysostosis and whose prognosis is further complicated by a microcephalic condition, the ability to learn to communicate, especially in abstract comprehension, is a monumental task. And this represents only one combination of disorders which taxes the ingenuity of the teacher and the performance of the child.

Regardless of the area or areas of deficit, it becomes the responsibility of the teacher and school to provide appropriate opportunities to learn. One such method, utilizing the simultaneous sense training approach, has been successful in the acquisition of receptive and expressive language.

Through the integration and correlation of the visual-auditory-kinesthetic and motor systems, the child with language inadequacies, although unable to tell about his experiences, is able to demonstrate comprehension by doing. As audition and speech are simultaneously introduced and incorporated with the visuomotor, the child has an opportunity to use all the learning tools, i.e. vision, audition, movement, nad verbalization. In addition to the previously mentioned gains, foundations of academic readiness are established by providing the child with an instant sight vocabulary to which he can respond with continued success and immense satisfaction.

The following materials are required:

1. Heavy cardboard sheets 9 × 12 inches (amount depending on number of concepts introduced).

2. Heavy cardboard cards 3 × 8 inches (twice the number of cards above).

3. Colored pictures depicting specific actions (sketches, photographs, or pictures cut from magazines, eliminating unessential background).

4. Package of assorted colored construction paper.

5. One black felt pen.

6. Rubber cement.

7. A box of plastic wrap or a can of clear plastic spray.

The following is the procedure for preparation of materials: (See Figure 12-1)

Figure 12-1. Picture-Word Cards, Action Form.

1. *Picture Cards.* On the heavy cardboard sheet, cement the picture of the action concept. Using the colored construction paper, cut out two-inch strips and mount as a border on the picture card. To insure permanency, protect each picture card by spraying with clear plastic or by encasing it in the plastic wrap, securely fastening it on the underside.

2. *Word Cards.* In the center of two of the heavy cardboard cards, letter the manuscript word representative of the action picture card. On one card, mount a ¾ inch border, the color to correspond with that used on the picture card. The remaining card receives no border. Spray or encase each in plastic wrap.

All other picture and word cards are prepared in a similar manner.

Further directions and notes for teachers are as follows:

1. Selection of the action (in order to relate to daily surroundings) is dependent on the environmental experiences of the child as well as his need for specific language.

2. The child should be positioned directly opposite the teacher. Remind the child to look at the lips and tongue of the teacher during the session. Point to the lips and the tongue as verbal direction is given.

3. Select an action picture card and place it before the child. Attempt to have him act out the activity spontaneously. Pantomime may be necessary to elicit response. If the child does not respond to the pantomime, actively demonstrate the task to be performed. Physically assisting the child in the performance of the activity may be necessary for appropriate response. Action should be repeated until positive comprehension is achieved.

4. After the initial completion and comprehension of the movement, hold up the color cued word card and orally exclaim the printed word, directing the child to focus his eyes on the lip and tongue movements. Then have the child match the word card to the picture card. Repeat the activity several times, allowing the child to place the word card on the picture card. Now verbally direct the child to perform the activity, holding up the word and picture for him to view.

5. Following the completion of the task, present to him a plain word card, again verbalizing the word, and have him match it to

the picture card and color cued companion. Once more the child is required to perform the motor activity. Remove the color cued word card from the picture card and have the child match the plain word card to the picture card. Repeat until comprehension is assured.

6. Remove the plain word card from the picture card and place the picture card face down. Display the plain word card to the child. Verbalize the word and attempt to elicit the appropriate vocalization from the child, calling attention to lip and tongue movements. Make several attempts.

7. Direct the child to perform the movement symbolized by the plain word card configuration. Review if comprehension of the printed form is not achieved.

8. Introduce each new movement as prescribed. Evaluate previously learned movements frequently to ascertain retention and recall ability.

A suggested variation to the above approach is as follows:

1. Hold up a selected action picture card before the child. Have the child perform the activity portrayed. To elicit response, pantomime may be necessary. If the child does not respond to the technique, actively demonstrate the movement to be performed. Physically assist, if necessary. Repeat until comprehension of the action is achieved.

2. Hold up another of the prepared action picture cards. Elicit response as previously described. At this point, attempt to elicit visual and motor discrimination. Any number of picture action cards may be introduced in this manner.

3. Utilizing the action form concepts introduced, hold up the corresponding color cued word card, exclaiming the name of the action. Draw attention to lip and tongue movements. Allow the child to match the color cued word card to the picture action card. Repeat several times. Verbally direct him to perform the activity, holding up both cards. Introduce the second and consecutive cards in like manner.

4. Now attempt discrimination among the selected action form cards and the color cued word cards by having the child perform the activity expressed by the picture and word. Review if discrimination process falls short.

5. Repeat the above two steps using the plain word cards. Do not remove the color cued card when initially matching the plain word card.

6. When all responses up to this point are satisfactorily expedited, remove the picture and color cued word card from view. Attempt to elicit the desired movements by holding up the plain word card and exclaiming the action. Discrimination among the plain printed cards is paramount. Review if comprehension has not been acquired.

Some suggested movement activities are

Bite	Eat	Run
Blow	Go	See
Bow (verb)	Hop	Spill
Come	Jump	Walk
Cry	Look	Wash
Drink	Play	Work
Dry	Ride	

PICTURE-WORD CARDS, ABSTRACT FORM

The purposes of the abstract form of the picture-word cards are to develop conceptualization of abstract commands, to coordinate visual-auditory-kinesthetic and motor systems as a foundation for symbolic interpretation, to develop the comprehension of visual abstract word configurations, to reduce concomitant emotional overlay by providing success experiences, and to provide a reading readiness foundation.

Here again, the child is offered the opportunity to engage in simultaneous learning experiences, utilizing abstract commands and word forms as a basis for conceptualization. Through the acting out of a specific pictorial situation, the child is able to demonstrate his understanding of the printed form and respond accordingly. Continued performance on this sensory motor level coordinates many acts basic to reading. Acceleration in the reading program is achieved since the child will have already learned numerous abstract word configurations which often constitute a reading stumbling block for those with language inadequacies.

The following materials are required:

1. Sheets of heavy cardboard 9 × 12 inches (amount depending on the number of concepts introduced).

2. Cards of heavy cardboard measuring 3 × 8 inches (twice the number of the cards above).

3. Colored pictures depicting abstract concepts. Illustrations may be photographs, pictures cut from magazines, or sketches depicting the required movements. The concepts listed below are initial suggestions, and it is assumed that the teacher will enlarge the list as prowess is acquired.

 a. *Up-down.* Illustrations depicting a child stepping up onto a wooden box and stepping down from the wooden box with the dominant foot.

 b. *Under-over.* Pictures exhibiting a child performing the movements of creeping under and over a "bridge."

 c. *Into-out of.* Pictures illustrating a child placing an object into and taking it out of a cardboard box.

 d. *Long-short.* A sheet of the 9 × 12 cardboard on which is mounted a long and short strip of medium fine sandpaper.

4. A packet of assorted colored construction paper.

5. One black felt pen and one red felt pen.

6. Rubber cement.

7. A box of plastic wrap.

8. A small, stable wooden box at least 9 inches high.

9. A cardboard box 8 × 10 × 6 inches.

10. A narrow strip of paper measuring 1 × 6 inches.

11. Medium fine sandpaper, one strip 2 × 12 inches and one strip 2 × 6 inches.

12. A board 1 × 12 inches, and 4 feet long.

The abstract picture-word cards are prepared in the following manner (see Figure 12-2):

1. Prepare pictures and words in the same manner as for the picture-word card, action form. In addition, on each picture draw a large red arrow to indicate the direction of the movement to be performed.

2. Holding the length of the 9 × 12 heavy cardboard sheet horizontally, mount the 12 inch strip of sandpaper one inch from

the top. Leaving a space of 3 inches, mount the second smaller sandpaper strip even with the left margin, directly beneath the larger strip.

3. Construct a "bridge" by supporting the wooden board between two chairs.

The teacher can illustrate the UP concept in the following manner:

1. Have the child positioned directly opposite the teacher. Remind him to look at the lips and tongue of the teacher during the session. Point to the lips and tongue as verbal direction is given.

2. Place before the child the abstract picture card depicting the concept UP. Have the child attempt to spontaneously carry out the activity, i.e. step up. Pantomime may be necessary to elicit proper response. If the child does not respond to this method, actively demonstrate the task to be performed. Physical assistance in the performance may be a requisite.

3. Following the initial completion of the step up activity, hold up the color cued word card and exclaim the word UP. Direct the child to focus his eyes on the lip and tongue movements. Now have the child match the word card to the abstract picture card. Allow the child to repeat the matching activity several times. Give the command "up" while holding the word and picture card for him to view.

4. Following the completion of the movement, introduce the plain word card, again verbalizing the word. Have the child match it to the picture card and the color cued companion. Once more require the child to "step up" onto the box. Remove the color cued word card from the picture card and have the child match the plain word card to the picture. Repeat until comprehension is assured.

5. Remove the word card UP from the picture card and place the picture card face down. Display the plain word card for the child. Verbalize the word and attempt to elicit the appropriate vocalization, calling attention to the lip and tongue movements. (To elicit the plosive quality, hold a narrow strip of paper vertically beneath the nostrils and have the child make the "puh-puh-puh" sound. Make several attempts.)

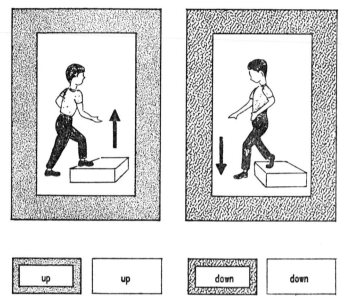

Figure 12-2. Picture-Word Cards, Abstract Form.

6. Display the plain word card and direct the child to perform the movement symbolized. Review if comprehension of the printed form has not been achieved.

The *down* concept can be taught using the following procedure. Utilizing all of the applicable directions and notes for teachers described in preceding sections, attempt to elicit the child's response in the performance of the appropriate activity. In stepping *down* make certain the child starts off with the dominant foot. For the initial "d" sound, have the child hold the tongue against the palate and make the sound of a woodpecker pecking in a tree—"di-di-di."

The *under-over* concept can be taught introducing each concept separately, beginning with *under*, and following the directions for the previous sections. Make certain the reciprocal pattern of the creeping movement, with eyes focused on a fixed object, is practiced.

To teach the *into-out of* concept, direct the child to first place the object into the box, then later take it out of the box. All previously stated directions that apply should be utilized.

The *long-short* concept can be illustrated by making use of the tactile and kinesthetic senses by having the child feel the length of the longer sandpaper strip and the shortness of the other. Apply the direction learned in other abstract concept areas. Hand guiding the child's direction, left to right, may be necessary.

Once basic concepts have been established, expand each category by introducing a wide variety of pictures depicting individual concepts. Such method will insure the child's overall comprehension.

PICTURE-WORD CARDS, OBJECT FORM

The purposes of the object form of the picture-word cards are to develop visual identification of environmental objects, to coordinate visual and auditory comprehension of objects with appropriate visual word configuration, and to provide success experiences to reduce concomitant emotional overlay.

Often the child is able to pantomime the use of various environmental objects yet unable to tell what the object is. Through the pictorial identification of the specific item and recognition of the accompanying word configuration, the child is provided a medium by which to communicate, temporarily bypassing the need to respond verbally. The underlying philosophy here stresses the acquisition initially of written (printed) form as a basis for language conceptualization, which stimulates and provides a foundation for oral communication.

All materials are the same as those used in the preparation of the picture word cards, action form. The object pictures may depict any item found in the child's home, school, or play environment. Color pictures are preferred. Eliminate all unessential background stimuli.

The object picture cards are prepared in the same manner as the action form. (See Fig. 12-3)

With the exception of the specific movements required in the action form, the same directions for instruction may be utilized. A list of initial consonant sounds are being offered here to assist the teacher in the auditory presentation.

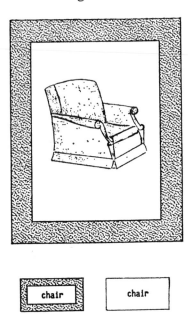

chair   chair

Figure 12-3.   Picture-Word Cards, Object Form.

m—Mosquito sound (continuous "mmm" sound). Have the child hold index finger against one nostril and continuously hum "mmm" as a mosquito.

s—Silly Snake sound ("sss"). Have the child fill his cheeks with air and slowly expel as a hissing snake. (Draw a silly looking snake shaped in an "S" form.)

l—Singing Lady sound ("lah-lah-lah"). Have the child lift his tongue up and behind the upper front teeth and sing "lah-lah-lah."

p—Motor Boat sound ("puh-puh-puh"). Give the child a narrow strip of paper, which is to be held vertically under the nostrils. Make the paper move by saying "puh-puh-puh," the motor boat sound.

j—Jumping Jim sound ("ju-ju-ju"). Jumping Jim is a frog who calls to his frog friends. With lips pushed together and tongue pressed against the teeth, he calls "ju-ju-ju."

r—Ready Rocket sound ("errrr"). Ready Rocket is poised on the launching pad, awaiting blast off time. 4-3-2-1-0, Blast Off! Child responds by providing rocket sound "errrr."

b—Babbling Baby sound ("buh-buh-buh"). Babbling Baby has not yet learned to say words. His only response is "buh-buh-buh."

n—Neighing Nellie sound ("neigh, neigh"). Nellie neighs "thank you" whenever someone gives her sugar. (Give the child a small piece of candy to elicit "neigh-neigh.")

sh—Shaking Shirley sound ("shhh"). Shaking Shirley will only stop shaking when someone holds his index finger vertically across his lips and says "shhhh."

d—Woody Woodpecker sound ("di-di-di"). Have the child hold tongue tightly against palate and make the sound of Woody Woodpecker pecking on a tree for insects.

ch—Train sound ("cha-chi-choo, cha-chi-choo"). Play train; have child alternately extend arms, first slowly, then more rapidly as the train picks up speed.

f—Funny Fish sound ("ffff"). Have child bite lower lip and blow a bubble as Funny Fish often does—"ffff."

v—Kazoo sound ("vvvv"). Place sheet of tissue paper over a comb and have child sing the "vvv" sound. (Make certain the child does not say "vee," just "vvv.")

t—Talking Tess sound ("ti-ti-ti"). Have the child imitate Tess who talks incessantly saying "ti-ti, ti-ti, ti, ti-ti, ti, ti-ti, ti, ti-ti, ti." (Concentrate on voice inflection.)

k—(Hard "c") Cold Crow sound ("cuh-cuh-cuh"). Show the child how to hold his tongue tip firmly below the front teeth. Cold Crow is so cold his tongue becomes stuck tightly under his bottom teeth and can only say soflty "cuh-cuh-cuh." (Soft "c") Has the same sound as "s."

g—(Hard "g") Goofy Goat sound ("guh-guh-guh"). Goofy Goat has a sore throat and cannot bleat. The only sound he can make is "guh-guh-guh" way back in his throat. (Soft "g") Has the same sound as "j."

h—Panting Boy ("hhhh"). Have the child pretend he has just completed a long fast foot race and is very tired. Show him how to breathe in deeply and pant.

w—Wind Sound ("oooo"). Have the child moisten his index finger. Using the unvoiced "o" sound, have the child feel the cooling effect of the wind on his finger.

th—(Voiced) Racing Car Sound ("thhhh"). With the tongue protruded slightly between the teeth, have the child hold his finger on his tongue tip and feel the roar of the racing car engine.

th—(Unvoiced) Radiator sound ("thhhh"). Have the child place his tongue just slightly between his teeth and then blow to feel the steam escaping from the radiator. (If steam radiators are available have the child feel the steam escaping from the safety valve, then allow him to feel his own escaping breath.)

z—Buzzing Bee sound ("zzzz"). Place between the child's teeth a narrow strip of paper. Have the child then pretend he is a bee and must say "zzzzzz" as he flies about looking for flowers.

y—Cowboy Yell ("yi-yi-yi"). Pretend to be cowboys. Straddle a chair and gallop away shouting "yi, yi, yi." (Wearing a cowboy hat may better set the stage.)

ng—Martian sound ("ing-ong-ung"). Have the child pretend he has just landed his space ship on Mars. As he climbs down from his space ship he meets a Martian creature who greets him with "ing-ong-ung."

CORRELATION CARDS

The purposes of the correlation cards are to develop symbolic relationships through matching activities, to develop visual recognition of environmental associations, and to integrate and correlate environmental associations with developmental speech and language.

For speech and language to manifest itself, it is paramount for the child to be able to relate and associate with his environment. Depending on the individual's physical, social, and cultural background, a variety of different experiences will be brought to the learning situation. It becomes the responsibility of the teacher to integrate and correlate these experiences within the framework of daily activity. The correlation cards are designed to associate known isolated and separate entities with a broader and more comprehensive category of organization. Through such organizational development, visual and auditory perception is made possible and a basis for language is achieved.

The following materials are required:

1. Heavy cardboard cards 9 × 12 inches (amount depending on number of associations desired).

2. Heavy cardboard strips 9 × 12 inches (amount to correspond with the number of 9 × 12 cards).

3. Heavy cardboard cards 2 × 3 inches (an indefinite number, amount depending on number of associations per correlation card).

4. *Object card*:
   a. Large colored picture depicting a specific object, i.e. a hat.
   b. Duplicate picture, 2 × 3 inches, of the object depicted on the larger card.
   c. Homomorphic pictures, 2 × 3 inches, but not duplicates of the object (pictures that vary in a number of ways,—shape, color, size, design).

5. *Scene card*:
   a. Colored picture portraying a real and valid environmental scene, i.e. a child in a sandbox surrounded by a number of playthings.
   b. Duplicate pictures of the individual items depicted in the scene.
   c. Homomorphic pictures, but not duplicates of the individual items—pictures that are similar yet different, i.e. a shovel is a shovel regardless of shape, size, or function.

6. Roll of 1 inch masking or transparent tape.

7. Rubber cement.

8. Can of clear plastic spray.

Materials are prepared in the following manner (see Figs. 12-4 and 12-5):

1. *Object and scene cards.* At the bottom of the 9 × 12 cardboard card, securely fasten with tape the 9 × 12 inch cardboard strip to form a pocket.

2. On the 9 × 12 card, cement a picture of the desired object or environmental scene.

3. *Correlation cards.* Mount the duplicate and homomorphic pictures on the 2 × 3 inch heavy cardboard cards.

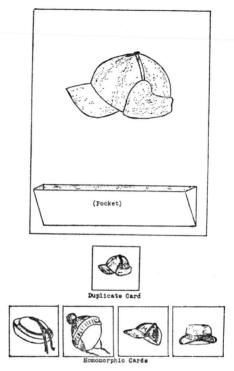

Figure 12-4. Correlation Cards, Object Form.

4. To insure permanency, spray all prepared cards with the clear plastic spray.

Position the child directly opposite the teacher and place before him one of the cards depicting the object or scene. Do not, at this time, reveal the correlation card. Discuss the pictured concept. Pantomime, both on the part of the child and teacher, to elicit response and comprehension is acceptable.

Select one of the duplicate correlation cards and, holding it at mouth level, direct the child to look at the teacher's lip and tongue movements. After repeating the name of the item on the correlation card several times, have the child attempt to reproduce the name. Accept his honest attempt by expressing glee and enthusiasm and be conscious of the fact that the activity is not a speech therapy session. Introduce each of the cards in like manner and have him first match and then place each into the

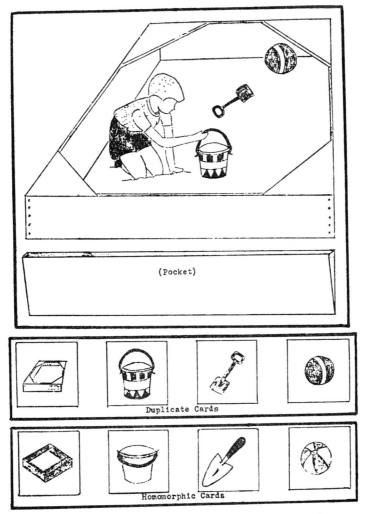

Figure 12-5.   Correlation Cards, Scene Form.

pocket of the object or scene card. Repeat the activity until comprehension is assured.

Place the same object or scene card before the child and lay out the appropriate correlation cards intermingled with cards of inappropriate items. Have the child select and match the correlation cards to the object or scene card, then slip it into the pocket. Note errors and repeat the developmental steps, if necessary. Following the mastery of matching the duplicate correlation cards, introduce the homomorphic cards in the manner previously prescribed.

Each new object, environmental scene, and correlation material is to be introduced as outlined. Object cards, because of their relative simplicity, precede the scene cards. Initial scene cards should depict only a few items, progressing to an increased number as prowess develops. Learned concepts are to be evaluated frequently to assure retention and recall ability.

Selected objects are as follows:

Baby	Dog
Ball	House
Book	Lady
Boy	Man
Cat	Girl
Doll	Tree

Suggested environmental scenes are as follows:

Classroom (school)	Rooms in the Home
Circus	Sandbox
Farm	Seashore
Firehouse	Service Station
Playground	Supermarket (store)
Picnic	Zoo

TIME ACTIVITY CARDS

The purposes of the time activity cards are to provide the child with external structure for direction in daily activities, to develop the sequence of time as applied to the concepts NOW and AFTER, and to reduce emotionally charged issues by providing pattern and routine.

Frequently the child who has a receptive and expressive communication disorder experiences difficulty comprehending the time sequence of daily activities. The resultant effect of this inability is often manifested in negative response. The child may refuse to participate in a specific activity because he feels it is not the proper time, he may resent any change in daily schedule which he is unable to comprehend, or he may become apprehensive because he does not know what is expected of him. Through the use of the time activity cards, the child is able to regiment himself to time sequence and routine in a serene and stable manner.

Although the time activity card instruction is generally initiated in the school, it should be extended to encompass all of the child's daily activities. Proper home-school relationship and the enthusiasm of the parent to assist are paramount to the establishment of the child's structure and control.

The following materials are needed (See Fig. 12-6).

1. Heavy cardboard 9 × 12 inches (number depending on activities introduced).

2. Individual drawings of the child engaged in activities relevant to his daily environment and schedule. (Account for individual and environmental differences in the selection of the activities.)

3. Heavy cardboard cards, 3 × 8 inches (indefinite number).

4. Package of assorted colored construction paper.

5. One black felt pen.

6. Rubber cement.

7. Can of clear plastic spray.

Preparation of materials is as follows:

1. On the 9 × 12 cardboard sheet, using the black felt pen draw an outline sketch of the desired physical environment.

2. Utilize construction paper of various colors to depict the human image, i.e. a red skirt, a yellow blouse, and brown hair.

3. Adhere the human image parts to the environmental sketch.

4. Print the word NOW on one of the 3 × 8 cards. On all others, print the word AFTER. The total number of cards printed with AFTER should correspond to the total number of the time activity cards.

5. In the upper left hand corner of the activity card, construct a clock face 3 inches in diameter. Placement of the clock hands is dependent on the time the activity occurs.

6. Spray each card with clear plastic to insure permanency.

Select the time activity card representing the current activity

Figure 12-6.   Time Activity Cards.

and place it before the child. Using simultaneous language and pantomime and drawing attention to the clock hands on the card and the hands on the wall clock, indicate that NOW is the time for the activity. Take the word card NOW and place it directly below the activity card.

Beside the current activity card, place all the remaining activity cards in the desired time sequence. Below each, place one of the AFTER word cards. Again, simultaneously using language and pantomime and drawing attention to the hands of the clock, emphasize the AFTER activities. Repeat until comprehension is assured.

Introduce the second activity of the day in similar fashion, eliminating the initial time activity card from view. Successive situations all follow the pattern outlined.

Preferably, cards should be propped or mounted against a bulletin board to afford the child with an overall view and visual explanation of the day's activities.

SUMMARY

The preceding communication activity skills have been an attempt to demonstrate the potentialities of simultaneous sensory motor training, an integrated and correlated perceptual process on which extended and future learnings depend. Although the concept of simultaneous sensory motor training has been utilized here in the development and advancement of communication skills, its tenets are adaptable and applicable to all handicapped children and to many areas of physical and intellectual endeavor.

Chapter 13

TEACHING LANGUAGE PATTERNS

RUTH EDGINGTON

CHILDREN WITH LEARNING DISABILITIES in the area of language find traditional grammar as taught at the junior high school level a baffling experience. It seems to me that for these children the ability to write clear, straightforward sentences of ten or more words is a more functional objective. In general, these children are poor spellers who limit their written expression to words they think they can spell correctly. Usually, they have demonstrated that their ability to repeat rules from rote memory has little influence or carry-over into reading or into the spelling used in written expression.

Particularly striking examples are shown by those children who have difficulties in the reception of auditory-verbal data, its integration and/or retrieval for verbal expression. Their vocabularies are meager, aphasoid in quality, and concrete in meaning. By the time the junior high school level is reached, their efforts to use the increasingly abstract terminology and rules in grammar are but exercises in futility.

My first year of teaching orthopedically impaired children showed me the critical need for learning how to teach language better. It seemed to me the real masters of this art must be teachers of the deaf and partially deaf. I read several books, among which was Edith Fitzgerald's *Straight Language for the Deaf.* Although I was unable to get any formal training, I was drawn to the logic of her approach. On the basis of previous training, limited experience with hard-of-hearing children, and

Reprinted from the *Academic Therapy Quarterly,* Vol. 4 (1969), pp. 139-145. By permission of the author and publisher.

meager understanding of the Fitzgerald Key, I waded in, adapting this method to my hearing cildren who had language problems.

My success was less than I had envisioned, although the hard-of-hearing children definitely improved in language usage. Later, I worked more with older children in junior high school who were having learning disabilities. The clues were less obvious, but I was reminded of my younger children who had had greater difficulty in processing language. I plunged in again, making more adaptations and setting shorter-term goals. Results with these children, whose ability to learn auditorily was weak, showed greater facility in language usage.

Across one chalkboard I made a simplified form of the Fitzgerald Key for one group's English lesson (see Table 13-I.)

TABLE 13-I

	Who	Verb		Where	When
1.	John	was absent			yesterday.
2.	I	went		to Scouts	after school.
3.	Roger	walked		to my desk.	
4.	Bob and I	rode	our bicycles	downtown	Saturday.

I wrote the first sample sentence in answer to my oral question, "Who was absent yesterday?" The children read the sentence aloud and one of them asked why I put *yesterday* so far away from the rest of the words. Another student answered for me: "Can't you see she had to because that column says 'When'?" I reinforced his answer at once, verbally and with a big grin. I explained the other headings simply. Since the children already had an elementary concept of "verb," I used that word instead of the usual sign (=). Oral sentences in the same pattern were evoked and written down. The sentences were then copied for the day's spelling on the key paper given each youngster.

The next day we had several sentences about what had happened since school the previous day. (See Table 13-I, Sentence 2.) The spelling words for the week were designed to contain several common regular verbs in the past tense. I wrote these in sentences on individual cards which I gave to alternate class members as a "secret message." (For example, *Walk to my desk. Close the window.*) Each messenger had to act out his message for the other youngsters to guess, and the actions were recorded in the Key (Table 13-I, Sentence 3).

One boy wanted to write messages for our next lesson after copying the current day's sentences. Of course, I agreed that any of the class could do this and, in addition, they could choose to make up other sentences with these verbs if they didn't want to copy the sentences on the board. All chose to copy as a welcome change from the daily sentence writing with a portion of the spelling words. (Each English class grouping on the various levels wrote sentences daily, and soon other groups asked to use the key paper, too.)

The third day was a reception, with new message bearers. The fourth day, the rest of the spelling words were written in the regular way, after each boy had an opportunity to ask for class help with an oral sentence for any word he thought might prove troublesome. I repeated each sentence, pointing to its "key" position.

Friday, the final spelling day, showed a marked improvement in the group's attitude toward the test itself and in higher scores. In fact, the boys were a bit cocky about their gains. The other groups congratulated them and suggested the boys bring back their papers on Monday to put on the bulletin board. Not a single boy forgot to return his paper, and some parents had taken time to write a note of praise for their son's gain on the test paper.

Monday, at class time, the boys' interest was lively. After discussing the kind of words that had been in the *Who* column, it was decided that we would try telling about something someone else in the family did over the weekend. One boy volunteered a sentence (Table 13-I, Sentence 4), and as soon as I had written "our bicycles," he asked to write the rest. The other boys agreed he had put the words in the right places. He bragged a bit, saying, "I could have done it all if I had known where to put the part about the bicycles!" There was no lack of volunteer sentences that day, but no one else offered to write them on the board. However, each boy came up to read his sentence and point to the column headings as he read.

The story read Monday had been about unusual pets in several countries. The next day I suggested that the students could write about their own pets (past or present). You may be sure that the week's spelling words included some describing pets and their care, but the children thought it was a coincidence.

I wrote the word *What* under *Who* in the heading, explaining that *who* is saved for people and everything else is *what*. They thought this is a neat arrangement and no one asked why, fortunately for me, as I didn't think the group was ready for pronoun conventions at this point. The classwork went quickly and smoothly. Sentences were copied rapidly and about half the class wrote additional sentences which they thought of after the oral sentence time was over. Here, the tendency to perseverate worked well to produce sentence patterns in the same format.

The following day I wrote these extra sentences in the Key and the authors were allowed to read their own—a red-letter day for them. After further sentences were evoked by the stimulus of the previous sentences (time usually set a limit of seven to ten sentences a day), a bonus was given the authors, they could omit theirs from the rest when they copied. One or two more boys then wrote extras.

In the succeeding class period, the extra sentences served to introduce another refinement of a heading. "My dog's collar came unbuckled" caused the word *Whose* to be written between *Who* and *What*. A simple explanation was given and several more sentences in this new pattern were offered by others in the group. By this time, only three words remained unused in the week's lesson, and the boys finished making sentences with these words after copying from the board.

Friday brought another test day with equally satisfactory results, showing retention of previous gains. A teacher bonus was found in the sentences of the nonparticipants, several of whom considerably improved their sentence writing in length and complexity. On checking with one of them to account for his improvement, he grinned sheepishly and said, "I guess I've been listening a little." I assured him that he or anyone else was free to listen if he could spare the time and still get his work finished.

The third week, I decided to introduce color cuing. I selected construction paper to match the colored chalk writing of greatest visibility, cut a strip 1 to 1¼ inches wide, and fastened it with plasti-tac under each heading. The children decided on the colors for the headings: red for *Who* (the subject), orange for *Verb*, purple for *Where* (adverbial phrase of time), and finally I put the remaining color, yellow, in the column without a heading (indirect and direct object). This column was purposely left blank to avoid confusion among terms (*what-whom, whom-whose-what*) for indirect and direct object with the terms used in the subject column.

Monday, before school, the colored strips were in place with matching colored chalk under each column. At the start of class I wrote the first sentence (see Table 13-II) and then read it aloud, making each word with cue colors. I pointed out that the colors would help us remember the Key more easily. Other sentences were then volunteered. Instead of copying these sentences, the children were given narrow strips, 3 to 4 inches wide, with the following headings: *Who, Whose, What* (underlined in red), *Verb* (underlined in orange), *Where* (underlined in purple), and *When* (underlined in green).

From the day's sentences two examples were chosen for each strip and underlined with the appropriate colors. The assignment was to think of five more words or phrases for each strip. One boy asked if he could look in his speller when he ran out of examples. As he had asked me privately, I agreed it was a good idea, provided he use the definition section at the back of the speller and that he understood how to use the abbreviations and the various meanings. I took him aside later and had him show me how he found the two examples (not in previous spelling lessons) and how he knew which strip to put them on. He proved to me he had used the cues in the definitions correctly. He agreed to keep this resource a secret until later, when the others were ready and would not be confused by the new and more advanced technique.

The next day, the strips were examined by pupil partners. Any

TABLE 13-II

MODIFIED FITZGERALD KEY[1]

These sentences are samples from several lessons, each word or phrase being underlined with its own cue color.

Who Whose What	Verb			Where	From How long For How often With How much How Why	When
(red)	(orange)	(yellow)	(purple)		(brown)	(green)
I	went			to the show		last night.
Joe	went swimming					Sunday.
The cat	hurt		his paw.			
The dog	likes		his bone.			
Mother's hat	is pretty,					
Keith's book	is			in his desk.		
A bird	flew			into the room		yesterday.
Tommy	gave		me his book.			
John	runs fast.					
Charles	went			to the store	for his parents	Saturday.

[1] Used by permission of the Volta Bureau for the Deaf, Washington, D. C.

differences in opinion were arbitrated by me or another set of partners whose lists were correct.

The slips were handed in by colors and shuffled. Each type was distributed to other children who had not seen them before. A short thinking period was declared so that each child could composed a sentence from the strips he had received. These sentences were written on the chalkboard in the Key and were color cued. The youngsters were given a choice of copying one sentence (not his own) from the board and adding three more of his own composition from the lists he had at hand, or he could make up his own. A few children still needed extra help from me. The resulting sentences indicated the youngsters' readiness for using the object column the following day.

The next day's class had a new problem to solve. Slips of paper with sentences containing commands were passed out. Examples: *Show Ben your arithmetic book. Give me a red crayon. Write your name on the board.* As each student's name was called, he performed the act indicated. Another student could volunteer to write a sentence about what happened (in the Key on the chalkboard). Another student read the sentence, adding color cues as he proceeded.

I called first on Ben, the most able student in the class, who automatically wrote the objects *me* and *his arithmetic book* in the correct columns. The rest of the students took this cue and experienced no difficulty, which astonished me so that I abandoned my planned explanation. I saved these sentences for the next day's lesson, as a reference source.

Wednesday's classwork, instead of copying, consisted of dividing the week's spelling list for the current day's and the next day's lessons. On Thursday, Joe asked if he had to use key paper, or if he could try using his notebook paper if he color cued it correctly. Ben wanted to try doing the same thing, saying he would go back to the key paper if his work wasn't right. I praised Wednesday's work again and said anyone might try Ben's idea if he wished. Three or four other students tried also. Only one youngster had to go back to the key paper.

Friday's tests again showed that the previous gains were maintained or some further gains made.

Beginning with the fourth week, the other students gradually followed the examples of Joe and Ben of substituting notebook paper for keyed paper. Each student had a similar trial period granted as an acknowledgment of continued successes in daily classwork during the ensuing weeks. Sustained success at this level was rewarded with increasing recognition and peer respect.

On the fifth week, the substitution of pronouns for nouns was introduced. On Monday, the previous reading lesson was examined in the English class. I read the lesson aloud, pausing after each pronoun for students to supply the antecedents orally. The spelling list was divided for the Monday through Thursday sentences to be written with color cues. In cases of doubt I was there to help the children. Tuesday's class time was devoted to making sentences using pronouns written in the Key.

Wednesday I read another story on the class level and one at primer level, asking the pupils to listen carefully for differences in the two stories and how they sounded. I had chosen two stories about going from an urban to a rural area and the different things seen in each area. The students' comments on the differences in style were recorded. It was determined that the higher level story was more interesting, less babyish, and had longer sentences that gave more information. Extra time for expansion in language use was taken for adjectives and adverbs, singly or in prepositional phrases. Suggestions for expansion were gained from studying the column headings. In using pronouns, such as *we, our, they,* compound subjects and plural verbs were also introduced.

On Thursday, library books on primer and fourth-grade levels were examined for further clues as to differences. Each student chose one book on each level from which he was to read five pages. One of the first differences noticed was in the number of pictures used. The reasons for this were explored and, before long, one boy mentioned that the upper-level books used words instead of pictures to describe people and objects. Another boy remarked that the little kids reading the baby books couldn't read the harder words, but that his class could. I wrote some simple sentences in the Key which were then expanded through pupil suggestions to more complex sentences. For example, *He rode in the wagon* gradually became *The little boy next door rode around the block in his new red and white wagon.*

On the sixth week, I put color cued lines where words from the weekly spelling list might be appropriate. (Weekly spelling lists were composed of words on the children's levels and grouped by the English classwork for the week.) For example:

	went		,
(red)		(purple)	(green)

	hit		
(red)		(yellow)	(yellow)

with a_____.
(brown)

The coach_____Tom_____.
              (orange)   (purple)

locker room_____.
(brown or green)

The color of the lines cued the children to the correct part of the Key for completion of sentence patterns in a prescribed way. By the end of the week they were thinking of themselves as "sentence doctors writing prescriptions" for me.

While it was very gratifying to me that the goals I had originally set were met and even exceeded by several students, my greatest satisfaction was in seeing the students gain self-esteem and respect for each other's progress. While individual groups of children will proceed at different rates, necessitating changes in the amount of reinforcement required, the results may prove equally agreeable.

I would like to invite readers to send me accounts of their experiments in expressive language improvement on either the elementary or secondary level.

REFERENCES

1. Alvarez, Adoracion A.: *Guide for the Teacher of the Deaf.* Devils Lake, North Dakota School for the Deaf, 1968.
2. Fitzgerald, Edith: *Straight Language for the Deaf.* Washington, Volta Bureau, 1954.
3. Paul, Jeanne, and Schneider, Nadine: *Color and Symbol in Language Teaching: The California Palms Supplement.* Riverside, California School for the Deaf, n.d.
4. Pugh, Bessie L.: *Steps in Language Development for the Deaf.* Washington, Volta Bureau, n.d.
5. Roberts, Paul: *The Roberts English Series, Books 4 and 5.* New York, Harcourt, Brace and World, 1966.

SECTION F

BASIC SKILL DEFICITS

Chapter 14

TREATMENT APPROACHES TO DYSLEXIA

Doris J. Johnson

A T A RECENT MEETING concerned with the education of exceptional children it was suggested that we first define our raw material before discussing approaches to remediation. The point is well taken and should be considered here since the term "dyslexia" is used to represent various conditions. The word itself means an inability or partial inability to read; however, there are many reasons for learning failure so a more specific definition is needed. In our work at the Institute for Language Disorders the term dyslexia is used to designate a subgroup within a larger population of children who have learning disabilities. A child with a learning disability has a disturbance in one or more basic psychological processes such as perception, memory, symbolization, or conceptualization. The disturbance may be manifested in the child's inability to comprehend or use the spoken word, to read, write, calculate, or perform certain nonverbal functions. It does not include those children who have sensory impairments, mental retardation, primary emotional disturbance, nor those who have had limited opportunities for learning. According to this definition, the dyslexic has at least average intelligence, has normal hearing and vision, has had opportunities for learning, and is reasonably well adjusted, despite his difficulties in reading.

The evaluation of children with learning disabilities requires the competencies of many professional persons including psychologists, pediatricians, neurologists, ophthalmologists, social work-

Reprinted from the *International Reading Association: Conference Proceedings*, Vol. 13 (1969), pp. 95-102. By permission of the author and publisher.

ers, educators, and others. The primary task of the team is to determine why the child is not learning. The intensive psycho-educational study is designed to explore the ways in which the child learns or fails to learn. It is concerned with learning processes. An important contribution to these studies is the semiautonomous systems concept of Hebb.[1] This concept proposes that the brain is made up of semi-independent systems, and that at times a given system, such as the auditory or the visual system, functions semi-independently from others. At times one system functions in a supplementary way with another, and at times all systems function interrelatedly. Diagnostically and educationally this concept has many implications.[3] Each psychosensory system must be appraised as it functions semiautonomously, in coordination with another system, and as all of the systems function simultaneously. In learning, this means that we try to ascertain whether a child can perceive, remember, and interpret what he hears, sees, or feels. We also explore the ways in which the systems work together. This being the case, we have suggested that three types of learning must be evaluated: (1) *intrasensory* learning requiring only one system such as audition or vision, (2) *intersensory* learning requiring two or more but not all systems, and (3) *integrative* learning requiring all systems functioning as a unit. The study of each type of learning includes measures of perception, memory, symbolization, and other basic psychological functions. Since reading is a highly complex symbol system involving many of these processes, it is understandable that the dyslexics constitute one of the largest subgroups within the learning disability population.

In normal learning all functions and processes seem to be related. If a child hears, we expect him to understand; if he can read silently, we expect him to read orally; if he reads single words, we expect him to read the same words in context; if he spells aloud, we expect him to write. These same assumptions, however, cannot be made in regard to children with learning disabilities. The interrelation of abilities varies greatly in dyslexics as compared with normal chlidren.[5] Some have superior auditory abilities but very poor visual abilities; others, the reverse. Some have adequate intrasensory abilities but poor intersensory or integrative functions. They perceive and remember what they hear or see, but they cannot associate the information from two or more sensory channels simultaneously. Some have adequate input but poor output; they comprehend but cannot express themselves. In some a specific mode of output such as writing or speaking may be impaired. Because of these variations in abilities we must examine tasks given to children according to a process orientation. Rather than noting only grade levels on achievement tests, we must examine the child's performance in relation to the processes that were required. For example, a ten-year-old boy reads silently at the fourth grade level but only at a second grade level orally. An inspection of the processes required for each task indicates that the silent reading test requires only intrasensory visual functions whereas the oral requires both auditory and visual. In contrast, a seventh grade boy comprehends *only* when he reads aloud. He must go through an auditory translation in order to interpret visual symbols. Discrepancies of this type may also be noted in spelling achievement. The processes involved in multiple choice, oral, and dictated spelling tests are so different that children manifest differences of three or four grades, depending upon their specific learning deficits.

A major purpose for analyzing systems and processes is to determine which learning circuits are operative or inoperative. A second is to determine what and how the child should be taught. If a student reads silently, our task is not to teach him to read per se, but to help him "reauditorize" words. Similarly, if he spells better orally we would try to help him "revisualize" letters or form the visual-motor patterns for writing. When working with a dyslexic, we attempt to analyze the child's strengths and weaknesses, and then select methods which correspond with his learning patterns.

In our research, diagnosis, and remediation, we have emphasized another basic concept called *overloading*. Many children fail to learn, or become confused if they are required to assimilate information through more than one system at a time. Some can look and learn or can listen and learn, but they cannot look, listen, *and* learn. The information being received through a given sensory modality impedes integration of the information being received through another. Overloading may be seen clinically in the child's failure to learn, his confusion, his random movements, and occasionally by behavior resembling seizures. The concept of overloading has considerable relevance for teaching dyslexics. If a multisensory or VAKT approach is used inappropriately, learning may actually be impeded.

To explore the factor of overloading in relation to learning, we are engaged in making brain studies. While the child is engaged in learning tasks (intrasensory, intersensory, and integrative), EEG's are taken and analyzed by computer techniques. The presumption is that we will be able to explore the concept of overloading as it relates to dyslexia and other learning disabilities. Hopefully, our educational methods, techniques, and procedures can be more scientifically oriented in the future. Conceivably, research will reveal that some children learn only in the presence of certain well defined conditions of input and output.

Although the goal is to teach all dyslexics to read, the initial approach varies with the nature of the disability. Many fall into one of two major categories—those who are deficient in visual processes and those who are deficient in auditory learning. We have called the former group visual dyslexics. Characteristically they have a tendency to reverse, rotate, or invert letters or transpose letters with words. Some attend to details within words or to the general configuration but not to both. Some have a reduced rate of visual perception. Most have visual memory problems which prevent them from remembering whole words. As Hinshelwood[2] stated many years ago, certain children seem to be capable of storing auditory but not visual images. Because they cannot perceive and remember whole words, we use an elemental or phonic approach in remediation. Letter sounds are introduced (a few consonants and short vowels) and the student blends them into meaningful words. Letter names are not used in the early stages and few if any rules are used. Rarely are associations such as *a* for *apple* used. The objective is to help the student unlock the code, to convert the visual to the auditory as simply as possbile. The forms of the letters should be kept constant since the visual dyslexic often finds it difficult to read both upper and lower case print. As soon as he can attack several words consistently, phrases and sentences are presented. A few sight words such as *the, you,* and *I* are introduced in context so the sentences can be natural and similar to the child's spoken language. In this way he can begin to anticipate words while reading. Although some of the current linguistic readers have a vocabulary which is appropriate for this group (with consistent sound-symbol associations), the sentence structure in a few is distorted and confusing; hence, the children fail to acquire meaning.

The basic approach to reading for the visual dyslexic circumvents his basic weakness and capitalizes on the strengths; however, work is also done to improve the deficit. A two-pronged remediation plan is used. The objective is to assist the child in both word attack and instant recognition. In the past we found it was neither beneficial to bombard the deficit nor to raise all skills to a normal readiness level. Thus, the dual plan. However, even when working on a specific deficit such as visual perception or memory, one must consider the most effective teaching circuit. If a child cannot perceive letters in the normal way he probably will not benefit from being given worksheets designed to improve visual perception. The teacher must decide how the materials can be used so that the child can, in fact, see the similarities and differences. At times color cues may be used. In other instances the size of the letters may be increased. In other cases taction (kinesthesis) or extensive verbalization will be used to "lead the child's looking." The techniques are not selected at random, but are based on the child's pattern of strengths and weaknesses.

In contrast to the visual dyslexic, the auditory dyslexic usually cannot learn phonics and therefore is taught to read whole words. Characteristically these children have disturbances in auditory perception, rhyming, blending, analysis, and memory. Although gross discrimination may be adequate, the children fail to perceive sounds within words. Many have difficulty with oral reading. Because of these learning patterns, the children are taught with an intrasensory visual approach during the initial stages of remediation. They are taught a sight vocabulary which consists largely of nouns and verbs, that is words which can be associated with an object, experience, or picture. In this way no oral response is required. While some children benefit from saying the words aloud, others cannot concentrate on the visual image if they also must call up the auditory. Therefore, even when phrases and sentences are first introduced, the assignments are arranged so the child can match them with pictures rather than read them aloud. In some respects the approach is similar to that used in learning a foreign language. Words are often introduced in units such as foods, clothing, or transportation. Since no child can learn every word from visual memory, and since we want to help him with word attack, a dual approach is also used with this group. As soon as a child has a substantial sight vocabulary, every attempt is made to help him with the auditory skills so that he can decode unfamiliar words. Again, the teacher must ask, "How can I facilitate learning?" Consider the possibilities that might be used to improve auditory perception.

One alternative is intrasensory stimulation. Some children cannot listen and look. They automatically close their eyes or turn their heads when working on difficult auditory tasks. A six-year-old, for instance, could take a hearing test only when his eyes were closed. Although some children spontaneously develop strategies for learning, others need assistance from the teacher. Therefore, while working on rhyming, discrimination, blending, or other auditory tasks the child is asked to close his eyes. With this slight modification many can learn to hear similarities and differences in words.

Another possibility is intensification of the stimulus. Some teachers intuitively raise their voices when working with students who have auditory perceptual problems, and, in doing so, facilitate learning. Occasionally we give children portable, binaural amplifiers to use during brief periods of instruction. When the sound is amplified through the headsets, many can perceive units within words that they cannot detect under ordinary listening conditions. A seventh grade boy improved substantially in spelling when he decided to wear the amplifier while the teacher dictated words in class.

Frequently teachers utilize cues from other sensory modalities. For example, various types of visual aids are beneficial.

Some auditory dyslexics were able to perceive the rhyming parts of words only after they saw the similarities in their sight vocabularies. After children learned to match pictures with words, the teacher placed the words in groups, asking the children to find those that looked the same at the end. Following this procedure, they began to hear the similarities.

Other children profit from watching the position of the tongue, lips, and jaw of the speaker. Those who cannot hear the difference between words such as *pin* and *pan* are directed to watch the mouth of the speaker. On the other hand, some cannot follow a sequence of movements and are not aided by this type of visual clue.

Some students profit from taction or kinesthesis while working on auditory perception. However, again the nature of the stimulus will vary. Some learn to feel the position of the tongue and lips when they say words themselves; others feel cut out letters or words; others write the letters and learn to discriminate differences. In all instances the basic question raised by the teacher is, "How can I balance the input simulation to modify the child's behavior?"

Some children present totally different learning patterns. They may be deficient in both auditory and visual learning processes and, therefore, will not respond to any of the methods described here. Some will need more taction and possibly a multisensory approach. In any case we stress the need for selection of methods by choice, not chance. Every attempt is made to analyze the child's style of learning and match it with appropriate methods and procedures. This being the case, teachers need to be familiar with many approaches and particularly with the integrities required for learning according to each. Critical questions pertaining to methods include the following:

1. What is the nature of the input stimulation? Is it primarily visual; does it combine auditory and visual stimulation; are all sensory channels used simultaneously?

2. What is the expected response from the child? Is he expected to match figures or to mark something? Is he expected to give an oral response? Does he need to know how to write?

3. What is the nature of vocabulary? On what basis were the

words selected? How controlled is the vocabulary? Do the words have a consistent phoneme-grapheme relationship? How many meaningful words are used (specifically nouns and verbs)? Is the vocabulary useful to the student?

4. What is the nature of the sentence structure? Is it similar to the child's language? Is the sentence length beyond the range of his auditory memory span?

5. What is the nature of the content? Is the material in keeping with the child's level of experience and interest?

6. Does the method require deductive or inductive thought processes? Does the child work from the whole to the part or from the part to the whole?

In addition to the preceding questions the teacher analyzes reading books for other factors such as the size of print, the amount of material on a page, variations in letter case and size, spacing between words and lines, length of story, and nature of the pictures or illustrations.

These constitute but a few of the variables to consider when teaching dyslexic children. Others include level of intelligence, language, and experience. As we learn more about children and about learning processes, undoubtedly more variables will be included in the plan. In essence the dyslexic child may be likened to a special type of computer.[4] The computer has a potential capacity for processing information. However, it will not function properly unless fed with a particular program which satisfies the necessary criteria for production. A program which fits one computer will not necessarily work for one of a different type. Furthermore, an incorrect program will be rejected by the computer, and under no circumstances will the processing of information occur with that program. Like the computer, the dyslexic chlid will process information only when "fed" with the proper program. Although we have countless variables to control (and match) when dealing with something as complex as the human brain and the reading process, the years ahead can be exciting as we do try, in fact, to study and program the variables in a more systematic fashion.

REFERENCES

1. Hebb, D.: The semi-autonomous process: its nature and nurture. *Am Psychol, 18*:1, 16-27, 1963.
2. Hinshelwood, J.: *Congenital Word-Blindness.* London, H. K. Lewis, 1917.
3. Johnson, D. and Myklebust, H.: *Learning Disabilities: Educational Principles and Practices.* New York, Grune, and Stratton, 1967.
4. Katz, S.: Teaching Techniques for Dyslexics. Unpublished paper, Northwestern Univ., 1968.
5. Zigmond, N.: Intrasensory and Intersensory Processes in Normal and Dyslexic Children. Unpublished doctoral dissertation, Northwestern Univ., 1966.

Chapter 15

TEACHING MATHEMATICS TO STUDENTS WITH LEARNING DISABILITIES

RONALD S. HOROWITZ

T EACHERS are often faced with students who do not learn, and often continue to use traditional teaching techniques that have failed. There are methods, however, which frequently prove successful, although they are considered unorthodox by many educators. These methods are based on some of the following assumptions, which are not meant to minimize the need for understanding basic mathematical concepts:

1. The basic assumption for students with a psychological block to mathematics is that a personal relationship of trust must be established first. Then, it is more appropriate to begin instruction with informal methods. A formal mathematics is sometimes the least appropriate way to initiate instruction.

2. Students learn from random and spontaneous experiences.

3. Popular games, hobbies, and releated activities can be a basis for instruction. Most popular games have survived because they are more interesting than "innovative" curriculum games.

4. A guide does not have to be a "package," but rather can be an outline from which many alternatives are selected for experimentation.

5. Techniques that are found to be successful in individual and small group instruction can often be integrated into a general classroom setting.

6. Memorization alone may hinder the student's ability to apply his knowledge in a new situation. Often, facts that are

Reprinted from the *Academic Therapy Quarterly*, Vol. 6 (1970), pp. 17-35. By permission of the author and publisher.

memorized are easily forgotten. But memorization associated with concept mastery facilitates transfer of knowledge.

7. The age of the student is not always an important factor in determining to what level he has advanced. Most of the methods suggested in this article can be adjusted to any age.

8. Instruction should not be initiated with a student unless he feels ready to begin; students will not learn if they sense that learning is forced on them by an arbitrary decision of a tutor.

This article is divided into three general sections: Part I is primarily for students who possess very limited arithmetic skills, and suggests games and related activities for motivational purposes. Part II contains important relationships that pertain to basic mathematical principles. Often, students memorize the techniques of basic mathematics but are unable to advance beyond an elementary level. Part III outlines some practical application of mathematics in areas that are, and always have been, vital to social acceptance.

PART I

If a student has intellectual potential, his failure to acquire basic mathematical skills is often due to a lack of readiness, ineffectual teaching, or a combination of both. The teacher misinterprets rote memorization to mean that the child understands the lesson, and subsequent material proves too difficult because the foundation was weak. A cycle of failure becomes a psychological block for all mathematics. Manipulations have often been introduced prematurely. Many students have progressed from $3 \times 5 = 15$ through $3a \cdot 5\,ab$ without understanding the concepts involved. The result of putting a cart of drill and memorization before the horse of understanding is that many students "tune out" mathematics.

Teachers and parents have been subjected to a barrage of cures. Traditional curriculum guides and recipe-lesson plans have been supplanted by the new math, and old wooden blocks have been renamed "rods." Rather than giving new answers, many of these approaches are based on memorization and manipulation. One cannot assume that because a learner remembers mathematical manipulations in relation to concrete objects such as rods that he understands the underlying concepts.

A similar fallacy is noted in the assumption that the more abstract words a student possesses, the more efficient and mature his thinking. When an abstract term is used, proof is required that specific meanings of the underlying concepts are understood.

There are other reasons why some students fail to understand arithmetic. Many teachers feel guilty when they do not follow the guidelines of a standard curriculum. Because of such factors as inadequate teacher training, large class size, and poor facilities, individual thought processes are often overlooked. Some students seem to answer a teacher's question as a quest for success in peer competitiveness, whether or not the answers are correct. Even an appropriate response is not always a clear indication of the child's grasp of the subject. In *How Children Fail*, John Holt states the following:

> We must not fool ourselves, as for years I fooled myself into thinking that guiding children to answer by carefully chosen leading questions in any respect is different from just telling them the answer in the first place. Children who have been led up to answers by teacher's questions are later helpless unless they can remember the questions or ask themselves similar questions, and this is exactly what they can't do. The only answer that really sticks in a child's mind is thse answer that he asked or might ask himself.[4]

Before proceeding to outline some methods and procedures for a tutorial program, some important objectives which are essential in order to create a good learning situation are as follows:

1. Provide initial success for the student in the program of study.

2. Maintain a high-interest environment.

3. Look for areas of inadequacy, poor understanding of vocabulary and concepts as well as language problems.

4. Note inconsistencies in the student's thinking ability, such as ability to perform operations in a high-interest environment which are difficult in an academic setting. For example, it is interesting to observe children who play dominoes and cribbage well and yet have difficulty learning basic mathematics.

5. Decrease the levels of anxiety related to mathematical instruction.

6. Provide an environment that allows opportunities for questioning and decision-making.

Short attention span, distractability, and disinterest are sometimes used as reasons for why some children are not learning. These symptoms are often the result of boredom rather than what the child himself brings into the learning situation. It is fascinating to observe "highly distractable" children spending hours playing with pinball machines, cards, dice, and other games.

Substantive learning can occur within a framework of games, hobbies, crafts, and other self-stimulating media. Games provide a high motivational environment which develops the student's ability to deal with stress and complexity. Strategies in some games, for example, puzzles, crafts, will often suggest cause-effect relationships corresponding to formal mathematics. Experience has demonstrated that it is difficult to judge which games children can learn to play. It should not be assumed that because a child is poor in mathematics, he cannot learn complicated games.

Removing classroom formality is important to any new approach in mathematics. The relationship between the teacher and the student must take place in a relaxed atmosphere where basic mathematical concepts are incidently introduced. If students have encountered negative experiences in mathematics classrooms, a free environment can allow the teacher the opportunity to observe the student's thinking process in a relatively free setting. Applications of vocabulary meaning, discriminations, and relationships, can be observed.

Games provide opportunities for increased socialization, which is vital to students with learning disabilities. A thorough knowledge of the rules and concepts involved in indoor and outdoor games and activities is invaluable to all children.

Following is a suggested tutorial procedure for the use of games in teaching mathematics.

1. Ask the student to select items from the following List A (Stimulation Media) that he knows how to play and would be willing to play, or items that he would enjoy being taught.

2. Explain to the student that in exchange for playing the

LIST A: STIMULATION MEDIA

GAMES (G)

1. Chess
2. Draughts
3. Backgammon
4. Dice games
5. Checkers
6. Whist
7. Bridge
8. Cinch
9. Pinochle
10. Sixty-six
11. Hearts
12. Rummy
13. Casino
14. Solitaire
15. Cribbage
16. Poker
17. Bowling
18. Mahjong
19. W'ff'n Proof
20. On-sets
21. Monopoly
22. Yahtze
23. Parcheesi
24. Buzz
25. Simon Says
26. Shuffleboard
27. Follow the Dots
28. Lotto
29. Bingo
30. Hopscotch
31. Pencil games
32. Darts
33. Twenty-one
34. Pick-up Sticks
35. Baseball
36. Kickball
37. Dodgeball
38. Tennis
39. Badminton
40. Volleyball
41. Tetherball
42. Soccer
43. Field hockey
44. Basketball
45. Golf
46. Croquet
47. Relay games
48. Jumping games
49. Track events
50. Spud
51. Ice skating
52. Swimming
53. Fishing
54. Hunting

ACTIVITIES AND SKILLS (A)

1. Abacus
2. Map making
3. Graphing
4. Mixing chemical solutions
5. Designing house plans
6. Designing games
7. Operating cash registers
8. Puzzles and "fitting toys"
9. Stocks (actual or simulated manipulation)
10. Slide rule
11. Pedometer
12. Cooking (measuring cups)
13. Totaling and estimating
14. Restaurant tips

HOBBIES (H)

1. Model construction
2. Stamp collecting
3. Erector sets
4. Coin collecting
5. Photography
6. Sports (scoring, record keeping)
7. Number painting
8. Collecting historical data
9. Collecting match covers, baseball cards, etc.

LIST B: VOCABULARY DEVELOPMENT

VOCABULARY MEANINGS (V)

1. same
2. plus
3. none
4. many
5. whole
6. part
7. minus
8. next
9. beneath
10. round
11. group
12. nickel
13. subtract
14. quarter
15. one-half
16. set
17. inch
18. feet
19. yard
20. union
21. corner
22. meter
23. centimeter
24. dozen
25. allowance
26. fare
27. one-fourth
28. high
29. wide
30. a.m. and p.m.
31. dollar
32. per
33. cash
34. C.O.D.
35. down payment
36. installment
37. annual
38. semiannual
39. depth
40. quarterly
41. tax
42. collection
43. greater than
44. less than
45. digit
46. exact
47. zero
48. add
49. circular
50. dime
51. buck
52. multiply
53. divide

DISCRIMINATIONS

1. up, down
2. in, out
3. on, off
4. big, little
5. front, back
6. right, left
7. slow, fast
8. thick, thin
9. most, least
10. light, heavy
11. first, last
12. above, below
13. short, long
14. forward, backward
15. diagonal, across
16. all, none
17. empty, full
18. narrow, wide
19. more, less
20. few, many
21. quickly, slowly
22. less than, more than
23. large, small
24. top, bottom
25. in front of, behind
26. same, different
27. expensive, cheap
28. uptown, downtown
29. higher, lower

LIST B (continued)

RELATIONSHIPS (R)	ABILITIES (A)
1. color of objects	1. add and subtract with objects
2. number of objects	2. tell time
3. shape of objects	3. make change
4. conserving numbers	4. count by rote
5. conserving substance	5. read number symbols
6. comparing unequal sets	6. understanding money values
7. ordering size of objects	7. use ruler for measuring
8. relating sets of subsets	8. comprehend fractional concepts
9. "to" and "after" (relating to time)	9. add in columns
10. addition and multiplication	10. add two-place numbers
11. subtraction and division	11. subtract
12. hour and minute	12. identify money using decimal rotation
13. second and minute	13. totaling and estimating restaurant bills
14. ounce and pound	14. match time with daily activities
15. inch to foot	15. recognize number of elements in a group without counting
16. pint to quart	
17. nickel to dime	

various games, puzzles, and crafts that he selects, you will select others for him that you feel might be valuable for him to know.

3. Observe inaccurate and inconsistent applications of vocabulary meanings, relationships, and discrimination in List B (Vocabulary Development).

4. Teach the student the stimulation games that will most clearly meet the conceptual difficulties and insure opportunities to transfer concepts in new situations.

For example, a student might select checkers as one of the games he would be willing to play. The teacher would then select those items from List B that can be appropriately diagnosed and taught while playing checkers. He selects the following: (1) from *discrimination*—up and down, front and back, diagonal and across, in front of and behind; (2) from *relationships*—color of objects, number of objects, and comparing unequal sets: (3) from *abilities*—recognize number of elements in a group without counting.

While playing a game, the educational therapist should determine the student's understanding of the objectives; he should also be open to other problematic discriminations, vocabulary meanings, abilities. (To continue with the example of the game of checkers, the therapist finds that the student understands all objectives except the relationship between diagonal and across. During informal conversation, he also finds that the student does not understand distinctions involving money. The therapist decides to teach Monopoly and chess—from List A—in order to present the discriminations and relationships needed.) A teacher can be a catalyst to the thinking process by providing numerous alternatives for succeeding.

An additional point is that popular outdoor games direct the motion of the body into the learning of conceptual skills. Every child who participates in football or kickball makes use of mathematical discriminations and relationships. Arithmetic has to be learned in order to score bowling, football, and other games of skill, so why not use these abilities in teaching math.

An effective curriculum based on games is not simply playing games. Initially, the teacher's role is to find *any* game that the student enjoys playing, so that the student's mathematical level is determined. A common problem can result from offering too few alternatives, i.e. the student becomes bored. Attractive games to suit individual needs must be found. Another problem is that the students want to play games that are not ideally suited to the concepts to be studied. Most students will attempt the games you would like them to play if they are allowed stipulated periods when they can play the games of their choice.

Some students are intrigued by games where chance, not skill, determines the outcome. Even games with a high chance component, such as dice and some card games, contain many mathematical principles that can be utilized. However, the teacher should be aware of maintaining a balance between games of skill and games of chance.

The tutor may wish to develop a chart for the student, such as the one following.

STIMULATION-OBJECTIVE CHART

Stimulation Preferred	Development Objectives	Apparent Development Required	Stimulation
(Games selected by student)	(To be observed by tutor while playing)	(Vocabulary)	(Suggested and Taught)
G5 Checkers	D1 up, down D5 front, back D15 diagonal, across D25 in front of, behind R1 color of objects R2 number of objects R6 comparing unequal sets A15 recognize number of elements in a group without counting	D15 diagonal, across V7 minus	G1 Chess G21 Monopoly A1 add and subtract with objects
G21 Monopoly	V10 round V33 cash V35 down payment V36 installment V41 tax	A3 make change A6 understand money values	G29 Bingo A13 totaling and estimating restaurant bills

The approach in this section relies on the student's past mathematical knowledge, his personal experiences, and concrete objects as a basis for understanding concepts. Thus, it frees the teacher from presenting abstractions and allows him to think and teach as freely and realistically in mathematics as he would in other subjects.

Education rarely takes place when a teacher is talking too much, is ahead of, or is too slow for the student. This situation occurs frequently when a therapist feels compelled to use traditional lectures, kits, and guides, which are geared to the average student. Physical objects, such as blocks, rods, and games, are useful. The remedial therapist, however, must consider each individual's experiences and level of understanding.

It is possible to sustain the attention of virtually any student for five or possibly ten minutes. During this time, the teacher presents concepts, and the student is encouraged to give related examples from his own experience, from physical objects, and from past mathematical knowledge to explain or manipulate the concepts. He is also encouraged to participate in games that will stimulate his interests as well as improve his logic in important mathematical areas.

Following are suggestions for the presentation of a "formal" lesson.

1. After assessing the child's ability from diagnostic impressions, the teacher gives a five- to ten-minute lesson to the student. (Research has shown that it is better to start a student at a lower level, so that he can go forward successfully rather than make a premature beginning.)

Following the five-minute lesson, the therapist gives one or two appropriate examples to emphasize the mathematical ideas or concepts that were presented in the lesson. It is important to the success of this approach that the teacher not give explanations or examples that are purely manipulative.

2. The teacher elicits from the student three to five examples that are similar to the ones he has just presented.

He then asks key questions that will include the students to respond creatively: Can you show me ———? Can you think of ———? What things at home are shaped like ———? He also might ask the students to build three to five things that are alike, using objects in the classroom, such as blocks, rods, or chairs.

3. For the remainder of the time, the child is asked examples that demonstrate the property, idea, or concept presented in the lesson. Initially, if the student can't think abstractly, the therapist should give him concrete items with which to work, such as blocks, paper rods, bottle caps. When the child is able to give his own examples, he will be able to generalize from them and compare them to the principles being explained in the lesson. This process, however, should not be hurried. The teacher should not criticize the student's examples; he should try instead to understand the reasoning that produced them.

The teacher might follow the procedure for illustrated lessons given below:

The topic to be discussed today is the addition of fractions. I will give an example of two fractions being added:

Numerically $\frac{1}{4} + \frac{3}{4} = ?$

Example:

In the above example, it appears that $\frac{1}{4}$ of a glass of milk plus $\frac{3}{4}$ of a glass of milk is equal to 1 whole glass of milk, so that numerically $\frac{1}{4} + \frac{3}{4} = 1$.

Another Example:
(Pizza Pies)

Again, $\frac{1}{4}$ of a pizza added to $\frac{3}{4}$ of a pizza is the same as 1 whole pizza; this is another example which demonstrates that $\frac{1}{4} + \frac{3}{4} = 4/4$ or 1.

Homework question: Continue to create four more examples that will clearly demonstrate that $\frac{1}{4} + \frac{3}{4} = 1$.

The teacher might be able to elicit a few examples such as the following:

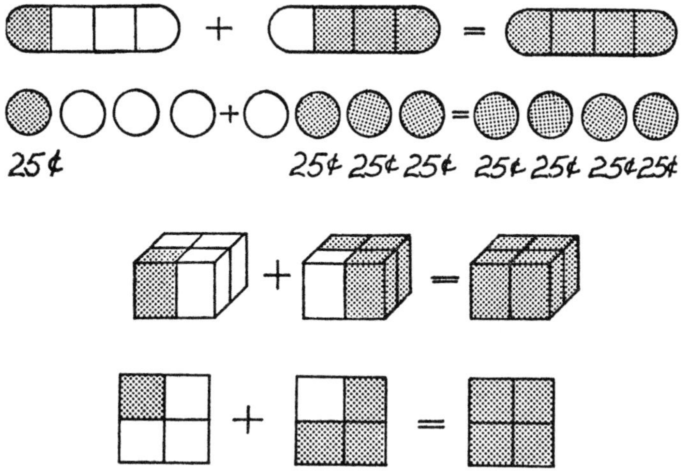
25¢
25¢ 25¢ 25¢
25¢ 25¢ 25¢ 25¢

The above examples reveal that the students have a clear notion of why $\frac{1}{4} + \frac{3}{4} = 1$. They could also be asked to give examples to show why $2/8 + 6/8 = 1$. After the students master this, one could continue to demonstrate $\frac{2}{5} + \frac{1}{5}$ and so on.

Some students, however, have difficulty thinking of any examples. "Fractional" pies, blocks, or some physical objects can help elicit examples.

The remedial therapist might find students giving the following examples to demonstrate $\frac{1}{4} + \frac{3}{4} = 1$.

0+000=0000

In the above situation, the therapist must review examples of fractional portions. For example, he might ask the student if he can draw $\frac{1}{4}$ of a circle. If he can, then the teacher could suggest that he use fractional parts to demonstrate the example given above. If he cannot, the therapist should show him several illustrations of what $\frac{1}{4}$ of an object looks like and then assign other examples.

PART II

The following curriculum is organized around addition, subtraction, multiplication, division of fractions, decimals, whole numbers, and some of their interrelationships. (The same techniques may be used for teaching areas of different content.) Each of the topics given below can be used as a basis for a five- to ten-minute lesson or series of lessons. Suggestions are also included to aid in the instruction of each topic. The therapist is encouraged to develop and create presentations in all areas to stimulate student participation. Unless students can cite examples to demonstrate the concepts, it should not be assumed that they understand even the most simple concept.

The teacher may find that the student cannot comprehend a particular concept or cannot proceed beyond a given level. He can then refer to the approach in Part I to search for misunderstood vocabulary, discriminations, or relationships.

Operation of Addition. Emphasize that *adding* and *plus* means "putting together," whether it be chairs, people, blocks, whole numbers, fractions, or decimals. Stress that in the process of addition, the order in which the sets of objects or numbers are placed together or added is unimportant. That is, five chairs plus one chair is the same as one chair plus five chairs, or $1 + 5 = 5 + 1$. In any examples that demonstrate addition, this condition will always be true. Some important vocabulary meanings are *plus, sum, total, more than,* and *greater than.*

Operation of Subtraction. Subtraction is the act of "taking away." A set of four books can be taken away, separated, or subtracted from a set of seven books. The result will always represent the number of objects left. It is also possible to cancel any subtraction with corresponding addition of the same quantity.

In subtraction, the order of operation is not reversible. In other words, $5 - 2 \neq 2 - 5$, or we can't take $5.00 away from $2.00 and arrive at the same conclusion as when we take $2.00 away from $5.00. The possibility of error in expressing a subtraction problem is much greater than in addition. Vocabulary distinctions include *less than, subtracted from,* and *minus.*

Operation of Multiplication. Multiplication is a series of additions; therefore, a firm knowledge of addition must precede.

When working with multiplication, it should be stressed that any multiplication problem can be expressed as an addition problem. For example, $3 \times 4 = 4 + 4 + 4$.

Since multiplication is an addition of equal groups, the order in which the numbers are multiplied is not important. For example, 3 times 5 blocks = 5 times 3 blocks. Comprehending words like *product, times, multiplier,* is essential.

Operation of Division. Subtraction is essential before division. Division can be viewed as a subtraction of equal groups. $6 \div 2 = ?$ The question asks how many sets of 2 there are in 6. The answer represents how many groups of 2 there are in 6. The students must undersatnd the terms involved in division. In other words, $8 \div 2 \neq 2 \div 8$. Since they mean different things, there must be literal translation of the division sign. For example, there are two groups of four objects in eight objects, but there are not two groups of eight objects in four objects.

Whole Numbers. (For primary school children.)

Fractions. Do not underestimate the difficulty that might be encountered with fractions. A lot of time should be devoted to making sure the student understands the most simple fractions. All students should be able to draw pictures to represent fractional portions. Their understanding should not be limited to the abstract.

When any fraction is presented, a student should be taken to a point where he can easily demonstrate three or four examples which would illustrate that particular fraction. For example, a teacher could begin with a notion that a pie can be divided into fourths and ask the student to produce similar examples.

Decimals. Decimals should not be attempted until fractional concepts are clear. Examples of fractions which are familiar to the experience of a student should be emphasized; some students might be familiar with baseball averages using decimals, others with test grades. If students can give you examples with which they are familiar, this will aid your teaching and their understanding. Be sure the students have a clear understanding of fractions and decimals. Above all, it should be emphasized that decimals are an easier way of dealing with fractions.

Relationship Between Addition and Multiplication. A multiplication problem might be presented and the student asked to express the same problem as an addition problem. For example, $2 \times 3 = 6$ might be shown, and then the student might be asked to express either $2 + 2 + 2 = 6$ or $3 + 3 = 6$ as being related addition problems.

Relationship Between Subtraction and Division. In the same manner that addition and multiplication are related, so are subtraction and division. If $6 \div 2 = 3$, this means that 2 can be subtracted from 6 exactly 3 times. Demonstrate how this works, using other examples.

Relationship Between Addition and Subtraction. Games of chance are good examples to use to demonstrate that addition and subtraction are reverse operations. If in flipping a coin, every time a head shows you win a penny (addition), and every time a tail turns up you lose a penny (subtraction), it could be illustrated that in the long run the addition and subtraction cancel each other. The students should be asked to create their own examples to demonstrate this relationship.

Relationship Between Multiplication and Division. If the above three concepts are clearly understood, the relationship between multiplication and division follows. Examples should be created to demonstrate why if $3 \times 3 = 9$, then $9 \div 3 = 3$. Again, good examples should first be presented by the teacher, then students should be asked for examples.

Relationship Between Whole Numbers and Fractions. The idea that all whole numbers can be expressed as fractions should be made clear. Any counting number over one can be placed into fractional form. In other words, $6 = 6/1$, $7 = 7/1$. The students should be helped to understand that as the numerators and denominators of fractions approach the same size, the fraction approaches 1. For example, $4/6$ is less than 1. $5/6$ is less than 1, but $6/6 = 1$.

Relationship Between Fractions and Decimals. The actual conversion of fractions is not of primary interest here. What should be stressed are concrete relationships. For example, the teacher might present a fraction such as ⅖ and draw a glass of water ⅖ filled and then ask the students what decimal would express the glass as being filled with that much water. If they were to respond .5 instead of .4, they would be very close, whereas an answer like 2.5 would show that they do not have a substantial realization of decimals. (In this case, they would have to be taken back to fractions.)

PART III

Some students experience little difficulty memorizing new rules but may be unable to interpret them. They may be able to add and subtract numbers successfully but not be able to count their change when purchasing an item. In such cases, the therapist can help the student to organize and classify similar experiences. Games and other activities associated with a topic can often be integrated with the instruction.

Sometimes it is necessary to overlearn a particular skill before one feels confident enough to progress to the next step. For example, a student who has problems counting to twenty is not ready for addition. The student will have to learn to count well before advancing.

A teacher should be alert to the youngster who can remember batting averages and keep track of bowling scores but cannot master a lesson in addition or subtraction. Here the problem might be psychological rather than academic.

It is often assumed that when mathematical topics are useful, for example, making change or counting money, they are easier to learn. But when students do not properly understand basic mathematics, even simple applications are difficult.

The listing in Appendix I is a model of how popular and commercial games (and their manufacturers in Appendix II), hobbies, skills, and activities can be related to basic mathematical topics. These relationships can be enhanced and the model expanded. Many applications can be supplemented by the procedure developed in Part I and the more formalized structures cited in Part II of this article.

The approach for teaching mathematics to children with learning disabilities presented in this article emphasizes the use of games and other high-motivational materials. While far from being comprehensive, the approach provides a guide, which is especially useful for children who have had negative experiences with mathematics. In the final analysis, however, the pupil-teacher relationship will determine the success or failure of this method.

APPENDIX I

Topic	Activity	Related Games, Hobbies, Skills	Commercial Games
Price of articles	Talking about prices of clothes, sports equipment, cars, and other items of interest; discussing what a fixed amount of money would purchase. Discussing simple tax problems, such as sales tax.	Operating cash registers and business machines Stocks (simulated or actual manipulation) Coin collecting Bingo (for prizes) Poker and other card games (for money or chips)	Catalogs Newspapers Magazines Billboards Advertisement
Weights and measurements	Discussing ounces, quarts, pints, gallons, and their relationships. Determining gas costs for a trip about the area. Using scales to weigh different objects and discussing relationship between liquid and solid weights. Also, talking about costs per lb. and ton of different products, ordering materials by mail (parcel post) to determine cost of postage per fixed weight.	Cooking Baking Mixing chemical solutions Photography (processing) Track events	Pi-O Math Labs Liquid Measure Set- Metric Liter Measure Meter Sticks Board Foot Cubic Foot Yardsticks Giant Ruler
Money	Relating the values of pennies, nickels, dimes, quarters, and dollars and "making change."	Monopoly Card games (for money or chips) Operating cash registers and business machines Coin collecting	

APPENDIX I (cont.)

Topic	Activity	Related Games, Hobbies, Skills	Commercial Games
Scoring	Learning how to keep score in athletic events and individual games.	Bridge Football Pinochle Basketball Hearts Golf Rummy Bowling Poker Dice games Twenty-one Whist Designing games	
Time	Telling time and discussing relationship between seconds, minutes, hours, days, and time zones. Distinguishing between a.m. and p.m. and calendar awareness, relationship recurrence of important holidays.	All games where specific time periods can be incorporated Relay games Mixing chemical solutions (and observing reaction times) Cooking and baking Photography (shutter speeds) Chess (using tournament clocks) Horoscope	Pendulum Clock Kit See-Through Alarm Clock Racemaster Stopwatch Sequential Calendar Time and Time Telling (text) Build-a-Clock
Large numbers	Discussing city, country, and minority-group populations, as well as significant economic statistics (millions, billions)	Basketball Running (five-hundred) Paper and pencil games Operating business machines Reading meters	Calculator Digi-Comp Structural Arithmetic Kits

APPENDIX I (cont.)

Topic	Activity	Related Games, Hobbies, Skills	Commercial Games
Comparing speeds	Comparing the relative speeds (miles/hour, feet/second) of birds, cars, airplanes.	Track and field events Swimming Skating	Magnetic Globe Game
Geometric shapes	Distinguishing between rectangles, squares, circles, triangles, and other common distinctions.	Chess Mahjong Monopoly Fitting toys and puzzles Model construction Hopscotch Dominoes Dice Cards	Shape-Sorting Box 300 Box Jigsaw Cone Rubber Fit-in Puzzles Wood Palm Puzzles Form Perception Box Giant Template Set Geometric Form Cards Shape Puzzles Shape Matching Series
Measuring	Develop practice problems which involve finding height, length, width, perimeter, area of rooms, and objects. Requires actual measurement. On maps, measuring distances between cities, reading scale of the map, plotting trips.	Map-making, map-reading Pedometer Paper and pencil games (involving measurement) Pin tail on donkey Construction tasks Fitting toys and puzzles Model construction Shuffleboard Designing house plans Golf Monopoly	Pedometer Measure-Up (text) Pi-Math Labs Math Projects: Map Making Color Dominoes Counting Box & Spindles Count-A-Line

APPENDIX II

MATERIALS AND SOURCES

Board Foot, Via-X Company, Los Angeles, Calif.
Build-a-Clock, Childcraft Equipment Co., Inc., New York, N. Y.
Calculator, Creative Playthings, Princeton, N. J.
Color Dominoes, Creative Playthings, Princeton, N. J.
Count-a-Line, Edukaid of Ridgewood, Ridgewood, N. J.
Counting Box & Spindles, A. Daigger and Company, Chicago, Ill.
Cubic Foot, Via-X Company, Los Angeles, Calif.
Digi-Comp, Childcraft Equipment Co., Inc., New York, N. Y.
Form Perception Box, Perception Development Research Associates, La Porte, Tex.
Giant Ruler, John C. Winston, Philadelphia, Pa.
Giant Template Set, Perception Development Research Associates, La Porte, Tex.
Jigsaw Cone, Creative Playthings, Princeton, N. J.
Liquid Measure Set—Metric, W. M. Welch Scientific Co., Chicago, Ill.
Liter Measure, W. M. Welch Scientific Co., Chicago, Ill.
Magnetic Globe Game, Childcraft Equipment Co., Inc., New York, N. Y.
Math Projects: Map Making, Book-Lab, Inc., Brooklyn, N. Y.
Measure Up (Text), Fearon Publishers, Inc., Palo Alto, Calif.
Meter Sticks, W. M. Welch Scientific Co., Chicago, Ill.
Pedometer, Creative Playthings, Princeton, N. J.
Pendulum Clock Kit, Creative Playthings, Princeton, N. J.
Pi-Math Labs, Creative Playthings, Princeton, N. J.
Pi-O Math Labs, Book-Lab, Inc., Brooklyn, N. Y.
Racemaster Stopwatch, Creative Playthings, Princeton, N. J.
Rubber Fit-in Puzzles, Book-Lab, Inc., Brooklyn, N. Y.
See-Through Alarm Clock, Creative Playthings, Princeton, N. J.
Sequential Calendar, Developmental Learning Materials, Chicago, Ill.
Shape Matching Series, Allied Educational Council, Galian, Mich.
Shape Puzzles, Developmental Learning Materials, Chicago, Ill.
Shape-Sorting Box, Creative Playthings, Princeton, N. J.
Structural Arithmetic Kits, Houghton Mifflin Company, Boston, Mass.
Time and Time-Telling (Text), Fearon Publishers, Inc., Palo Alto, Calif.
Wood Palm Puzzles, Creative Playthings, Princeton, N. J.
Yardsticks, W. M. Welch Scientific Co., Chicago, Ill.
300 Box, Creative Playthings, Princeton, N. J.

REFERENCES

General Objectives

1. Bruner, J. S.: *The Process of Education.* Cambridge, Harvard Univ., 1960.
2. Featherstone, Joseph: How children learn. *New Republic,* September 2, 1967.
3. *Goals for School Mathematics.* Report of the Cambridge Conference on School Mathematics. Boston, Houghton Mifflin, 1963.
4. Holt, John: *How Children Fail.* New York, Dell, 1964.
5. Kaplan, Jerome D.: Mathematical Objectives. Unpublished. New York, Institute for Developmental Studies, School of Education, New York Univ., 1966.
6. Neill, A. S.: *Summerhill: A Radical Approach to Child Rearing.* New York, Hart, 1960.
7. Paschal, Bill J.: A concerned teacher makes the difference. *Arithmetic Teacher, 13:*203-205, March 1966.

Information about Developments Pertaining to the Mathematics Curriculum

8. Ausubel, David P.: *The Psychology of Meaningful Verbal Learning.* New York, Grune and Stratton, 1963.
9. Beilin, Harry, and Gotkin, Lassar G.: Psychological Issues in the Development of Mathematics Curricula for Socially Disadvantaged Children. Unpublished. New York, Institute for Developmental Studies, Brooklyn College, 1964.
10. Berkeley, Edmund C.: *A Guide to Mathematics for the Intelligent Non-mathematician.* New York, Simon and Schuster, 1966.
11. Piaget, Jean: *The Child's Conception of Number.* New York, W. W. Norton, 1965.
12. Reed, Mary K.: Vocabulary Load of Certain State-Adopted Mathematics Textbooks, Grades 1-3. Doctoral dissertation, Univ. Southern California, Abstract No. 3706, January 1966.
13. Stern, Catherine: *Children Discover Arithmetic.* New York, Harper and Row, 1949.
14. Westcott, Alvin, and Smith, James: *Creative Teaching of Mathematics in the Elementary School.* Boston, Allyn and Bacon, 1967.

Practical Suggestions and Ideas

15. *Foundations of Learning.* A Resource Compendium for Teachers of Children with Learning Disabilities. Prepared by teachers enrolled in Special Education 5316, Univ. Arkansas Medical Center, April 1968.

16. May, Lola J.: *Mathematics Games for All Grades*. Darien, Teachers Publishing Corp., 1967.
17. Nuffield Mathematics Project: *I Do, and I Understand: Pictorial Representations and other teacher guides*. New York, John Wiley & Sons, 1967.
18. Russell, Robert W.: *A Program of Special Classes for Children with Learning Disabilities*. New Jersey Association for Brain Injured Children, 1964.
19. Wagner, Guy, Hosier, Max, and Gilloley, Laura: *Arithmetic Games and Activities*. Darien, Teachers Publishing Corp., 1968.

SOURCES FOR MATHEMATICS TEACHING AIDS

Book-Lab, Brooklyn, N. Y.
Developmental Learning Materials, Chicago, Ill
Edukaid of Ridgewood, Ridgewood, N. J.
Fearon Publishers, Inc., Palo Alto, Calif.
Humanitus Curriculum, Orange City, Florida
Mafex Associates, Inc., Johnstown, Pa.
Motivational Research, Inc., Maclean, Va.
Perception Development Research Associates, La Porte, Tex.
Science Research Associates, Inc., Chicago, Ill.

Chapter 16

REMEDIAL APPROACHES
TO HANDWRITING DYSFUNCTION

SHIRLEY LINN

To WRITE, a person must produce meaningful symbols on paper which communicate thoughts to others. This must occur in a manner that has meaning to both sender and receiver. Children with learning disabilities or a neurological impairment often have problems that interfere with the production of symbols which will communicate thoughts meaningfully.

Specific problems experienced by these children are poor construction of letters, such as lines which cross instead of meeting or which meet instead of crossing; corners which turn at irregular angles; lines which gape; poor or irregular letter size (some tall, some short, regardless of the size they should be); difficulty with letters which go above the line, below the line, and those which do both; reversals; inversions; poor spacing; poor placement or position on lines or between lines and spaces.

These errors are symptomatic of developmental lags or deficiency which may occur singly or in combination. They are usually associated with problems in such areas as motor development, language development (receptive, associative, or expressive), or visual perception. Writing itself is considered a motor skill, but it is one which is dependent on the ability of the individual to integrate separate skills into expressive action.

Traditionally, children are given lessons for handwriting which include oral directions by the teacher, illustrations on the chalkboard, writing in the air, and then application on paper at a desk.

Reprinted from the *Academic Therapy Quarterly*, Vol. 4 (1968), pp. 43-46. By permission of the author and publisher.

This approach assumes the child is capable of understanding directions which are given orally, illustrations which are given visually, and that he is also able to interpret and carry out the directions given. Carrying out directions is dependent on motor ability, the ability to perceive the space in which one lives and the space on which one writes, as well as the ability to translate oral directions into expressive action.

A child with learning disabilities is often unable to establish a keen understanding of directionality, laterality, or a concept of himself in his physical environment. Most children learn about their position in space throughout the movements of their body when they move, turn, crawl, pull up, walk and run. In every action, they should learn more about themselves in terms of space and their relationship to it. Children with developmental lag need assistance to learn to control and coordinate gross motor muscles. Remediation at this stage should include many experiences with their environment. For more complete assessment of the role of motor development and remediation, the reader is referred to the works of other authors.[1-5]

The problems of a student with an unstable understanding of himself in his environment are compounded when he is given directions for writing lessons. His understanding of directions for space-related activities is often limited. The words *up, down, slant, slide*, up until the time when he is told to sit at a desk and write, indicate directions in space oriented to his upright position. Once he sits at the desk, the words take on new meaning. The point of reference changes from the upright position to the horizontal plane on the desk. Children with learning disabilities, insecure in their own positions in space, are unable to make the transfer or understand the change in reference. Therefore, their ability to comprehend the directions may be deficient.

Remediation includes exercises which enable a child to learn to listen, comprehend, and then follow directions. They include orientation of the child toward understanding of names for places and places and positions in his environment in relation to his own position. Direct application of vocabulary to teach changes from upright to horizontal may be made by utilizing a hard surface, such as a tablet on a clipboard, which can be brought from the upright to the horizontal position gradually as lessons are taught. This, according to Frostig, enables a youngster to make the necessary transfer of vocabulary and its application from one position to another.[1]

Once control is gained in gross motor development, it should progress to finer muscles. Just as these children needed more structured activities to develop control over large muscles, they need structured activities to develop control over the fine muscles. They need more than the usual amount of experience with play activities, such as playing with blocks, simple puzzles, cars, dolls, and other typical preschool play activities. These activities assist in development of control over finer muscles.

Children who have difficulty with ordinary play activity receive little pleasure from it and tend to avoid it. This gives them even less opportunity to develop the skills that play activities promote. For children who do not learn to play naturally, it is often necessary to teach them as one would teach an academic activity. This involves study of the skills needed and a step-by-step presentation of the activity, being sure that each step is mastered before going on to the next. Once mastered, the activity is more enjoyable, is used more often, and in turn provides the needed practice.

As skill in preschool play activities improves, scribbling activities usually follow. As children master scribbling, they learn to match the visual trace with the lines made. They learn to produce lines, associate them with directions on paper, and to make the hands work independently of the eyes and the eyes work independently of the hands.

More structured activities often are necessary prior to the time writing can actually be taught. Children with lags in development need structured activities such as those provided by the Frostig Program for Development of Visual Perception. Especially helpful are the visual-motor coordination series. Children need to learn to listen to instructions which tell them to make lines in specific directions. These activities include verbal instructions which assist this development. As the child progresses through the worksheets, all important direction words are taught. Some children need even more emphasis on directions and their meaning. They need understanding of directions which relate to them personally. Directions such as, "Touch the bottom of the plate, the side closest to you," help children orient themselves to the space they are in and the space on which they are writing. Frequent review of directions, as the child sees them from his own focal point, is essential.

Difficulty in understanding directions and carrying them out is closely interwoven with the problems of motor coordination and visual perception. For example, children having difficulty seeing and making lines cross will receive help from visual-perceptual training in the areas of figure-ground. Also helpful is a good writing system which uses color cues. Children who make letters of all sorts of sizes and all over each space will benefit from exercises in sections relating to spatial relations, position in space, and perceptual constancy.[1]

It is important to give a great deal of thought to the writing system used. Many good systems are available today, but those which use color seem most effective. These cues seem to provide the stimulus to remain in the general vicinity of the appropriate place to write. They help children see when lines cross, intersect, and turn. One very good system is the *Peterson Directed Handwriting Series*, which uses color cues skillfully.[3] This series uses color to designate the area to be used for writing, black lines going across the page from left to right to show where letters are to be placed, colored lines showing directional differences, and directional arrows to show the way to make the strokes for letters. In addition, proper sequence of line construction is shown by giving the strokes numbers.

For some children, however, the color cues may be inadequate. Raised letters are sometimes needed for reinforcement through touching or tracing. This is often helpful with beginners as well as with children with persistent problems. Cards can be made to show how lines cross to form letters. First, letters are traced on cards with pencil. A thin line of glue is then used to trace the line, and yarn is placed on the glue. Variegated yarn can best provide the variety of color needed to coordinate colors of cards with the writing system used. When possible, children should make their own cards. In this way they can learn to see how lines cross, turn, and change directions in order to become meaningful symbols. Once complete, the cards can be used again and again for tracing. It is important to reduce the tactile structure as soon as possible so that it will not become a crutch. Tactile surfaces can be reduced by using only glue to outline the letters.

The system described above can assist children to see that different parts are used to make letters. Letters themselves should be combined to make words as soon as possible in order for the children to see that letters are parts of words and that they represent sounds.

To summarize, the ability to communicate with written symbols on paper is often a determining factor in whether a youngster is able to achieve academically or not. Children with otherwise normal ability are often unable to put their thoughts on paper, not because of thinking disorders, but rather because of writing disorders.

Until recently, writing disorders were considered primarily motor problems. With more study of motor and perceptual development, it has become evident that developmental lag can affect writing ability. Using this approach, it is possible to reach and work at the source of the problem, thereby reducing the incidence of a writing disability that becomes a permanent affliction rather than a temporary symptom.

REFERENCES

1. Frostig, Marianne, and Horne, David: *The Frostig Program for Development of Visual Perception.* Chicago, Follett, 1964.
2. Kephart, Newell C.: *The Slow Learner in the Classroom.* Columbus, C. E. Merrill, 1961.
3. *Peterson Directed Handwriting Series.* New York, Macmillan, 1968.
4. Radler, D. H., and Kephart, N. C.: *Success Through Play.* New York, Harper and Brothers, 1960.
5. Roach, Eugene G., and Kephart, N. C.: *The Purdue Perceptual Motor Survey.* Columbus, C. E. Merrill, 1966.

SECTION G

PROGRAMMING FOR
EFFECTIVE REMEDIATION

Chapter 17

TOWARD A TAXONOMY
OF CURRICULAR EXPERIENCES

John E. Bolen

ONE OF THE MOST PERPLEXING PROBLEMS in education is accommodating the different ways that children learn. In addition, there is but a scanty philosophical and psychological framework for developing instructional activities to alleviate this problem. Attempts by the schools to provide for learning differences in the classroom are often based on administrative expediency resulting in superficial treatment. The teacher is expected to offer activities suitable for the fast, average, and slow achiever. For maximum efficiency, she usually aims her instructional program at the average child. For the same reason, her source materials are geared for this level of instruction. Too often the slow achiever is left without a reasonable opportunity for successful experiences in the classroom.

Following is a proposal which attempts to provide the rationale and framework for developing kindergarten and primary grade classroom resource units to accommodate the various ways children learn. The theoretical constructs are those of Prof. Newell C. Kephart, formerly of the Achievement Center for Children, Purdue University, and presently Director of the Glenhaven Achievement Center, Ft. Collins, Colorado. The operational criteria and taxonomy for developing classroom resource units are those of the writer.

This schema is founded on the thesis that learning is hierarchical. The child's ability to engage successfully in higher mental

---

Reprinted from the *Journal of Learning Disabilities*, Vol. 3 (1970), pp. 247-251. By permission of the author and publisher.

processes depends greatly on the extent and degree that lower forms of experiences have been meaningful for him. Consequently a deficient background in motor and/or percept development may hinder the child from engaging in and profiting from higher level symbolic activities. Therefore, activities should be appropriate for the child's level of development and in a form which will enable him to assimilate information. Instructional units need to be flexible and comprehensive to accommodate the range of differences that are found in the classroom.

The structure of activities within the resource unit is the critical feature of this schema. The objective is to provide the slow, average, and fast achiever with appropriate experiences whereby each child, regardless of his developmental status, is working toward the acquisition of similar skills and understandings. There would be a common curricular objective for all, but the form of presentation would be different in terms of the child's stage of development.

To develop these common skills and understandings, unit activities in one or more of the following areas would be provided: (1) *perceptual-motor*—experiences which permit the child to explore his environment freely to obtain information; (2) *perceptual*—experiences which enable the child to integrate a variety of sensory information; and (3) *associative-conceptual* —experiences which permit the child to relate his percepts meaningfully, so that he can deal with abstractions rather than with things.

With such a system, instruction for all can be presented simultaneously at any level. At the same time that attention is directed toward activities to provide for the child's immediate development, curricula pertinent to his education are made available. Teaching does not depend on an arbitrary level of maturation or achievement; instruction begins immediately. Experiences are implemented through broad resource units that cut across subject area boundaries. Presentations within the unit are structured to provide the child with activities in the different learning levels to develop needed skills, and with ways to acquire knowledge and attitudes toward himself and his environment. These are outlined in Table 17-I.

TABLE 17-I

	Schema for Learning Experiences		
Learning Levels	*Skills*	*Knowledge*	*Attitudes*
1. Perceptual-motor (Identifying)	Perceptual-motor	Multi-sensory Approach	Self
2. Perceptual (Integrating)	Readiness	Exploratory	Social
3. Associative-conceptual (Interpreting)	Academic	Patterned	Work oriented

The following is an extension of Table 17-I. It serves as the rationale by which unit experiences are developed at the three learning levels.

PERCEPTUAL-MOTOR LEVEL

Perceptual-motor (Skill Area)

The child at this stage of development is in the process of establishing reliability between input (sensory or perceptual activities) and output (motor or muscular activities). A process in one of these areas will influence the other area. In teaching a particular skill, one cannot separate perceptual elements from motor elements. In addition, training in all aspects of the perceptual process must be given at one time. The child is engaged in varied motor experiences to develop his ability to make appropriate muscular responses to different kinds of stimuli. He is in the process of acquiring proficiency to cope with situations involving directional problems.[3] Experiences are also provided to develop his ability to use his body as a point of reference for organizing sensory data to structure his impressions. At the same time, the child is engaged in perceptual-motor exploration to obtain information relevant to curriculum content.

Multisensory Approach (Knowledge Area)

Learning tasks are structured in a variety of ways simultaneously for stimulating and activating one or more sense avenues.

Exploratory experiences are devised to provide variation in the task to broaden his perspective, and to prevent the child from becoming overly dependent upon one sensory avenue. The specific element of information and its presentation must be generalized and applied in a manner different from that in the original context.

Self (Attitudinal Area)

The child's attitudes and emotions toward the physical and social world are dependent upon a stable relationship of self to concrete objects. He engages in exploratory motor experiences to develop reliability of input and to acquire satisfying experiences which encourage him to explore new learning activities and social relationships.

PERCEPTUAL LEVEL

Readiness (Skill Area)

At this stage the child has an accumulation of stable experiences. Feedback from multisensory exploration is reliable. He is no longer preoccupied with the process of working through distortions in the perceptual-motor field and perfecting the skills involved in gross motor activity, eye-hand coordination, temporal-spatial translation, and form perception.[3] The objective now is to build upon these past experiences by the introduction of new activities for establishing the percepts needed to start a succession of impressions. The teacher must go beyond mere discussion, reading stories, or using visual aids to define an abstraction. The situation may warrant the interjection of real objects and events in order to activate as many sensory avenues as possible, and further stabilize the perceptual-motor bases described above. Language symbols help to establish nodal points for the development and identification of abstractions. Other important language-related skills included listening (the analysis and interpretation of various sounds and noises); following directions that include sequential manipulative steps; visual discrimination in distinguishing between objects, colors, pictures or geometric figures; dramatization and role interpretation;

engagement in oral language pursuits; and sorting, matching, counting, measuring, weighing, and identifying an assortment of objects. Traditionally, these readiness skills have been assumed as starting points for instructional purposes, and have therefore been excluded from educational programs, or left to maturation. However, mastery of these bedrock skills demand systematic instruction over a period of years.

Exploratory (Knowledge Area)

The child is given many opportunities to become involved in activities for manipulating and exploring the materials and equipment in the classroom, school, and neighborhood community. Because perceptions are based on the individual's accumulated experience, activities dealing with form, space, time movement, weight, number, social and aesthetic percepts are provided in a variety of related ways.

Social (Attitudinal Area)

At this stage, the child has developed a stable relationship between himself and his physical world. It is necessary that he be given freedom to explore the social world of the classroom because many important perceptions and attitudes are developed from these experiences. Liberal amounts of activities planned to permit social interaction need to be incorporated in the instructional program. Since each child is unique in his perceptions, his attitude differs from the attitudes of others in given situations. The teacher's role is to provide opportunities for the child to develop social percepts which can serve as a basis for more sophisticated judgments.

ASSOCIATIVE-CONCEPTUAL LEVEL

Academic (Skill Area)

The child at this level builds on readiness skills. He progresses from loosely organized associative activities to experiences which lead him to formulate organized concepts. He seeks interrelatedness in the information available to him through his existing skills and acquires new techniques for gaining more information.

In the classroom, opportunities to develop general process skills basic to many learning experiences must be provided. These include observational techniques, ways of collecting information, determinants for inclusion or exclusion of data, classifying schemes, and essentials for drawing conclusions and making predictions. Some activities are devised to teach for specific skill development and provide a setting for the utilization of these skills. A group of kindergarten children, after looking at picture books of animals and listening to animal stories, may dictate a chart story to the teacher. They may also be engaged in the transition from recognizing and writing isolated letters to grouping these symbols for word formation and perhaps to simple sentence construction. The curriculum in this stage remains open-ended and is essentially concerned with generating ideas to assemble into generalizations.

Patterned (Knowledge Area)

The child becomes consciously goal oriented as his skills become his tools. Experiences are provided which require the investigation of materials for satisfying his questions and interests. The teacher's responsibility is to teach for relatedness by presenting a wide variety of integrated experiences for developing associations and making inferences. The child should be given opportunities to process his information and guidance as he seeks solutions. His basic method of operation is to search for the relatedness in the information at his disposal.

Work-oriented (Attitudinal Area)

The child has now progressed beyond preoccupation with self. He does not need direct experience to develop new percepts. He can now learn vicariously. He explores his environment and is open to new experiences. He has developed strategies for processing data efficiently. The ability to persevere independently or work effectively in a group enterprise is being established. He pursues his tasks with some organization and purpose. He is able to sustain his interest without immediate feedback.

INSTRUCTIONAL UNITS

The resource unit is organized with regard to content, learning experiences, related materials, and behavioral objectives. The content and learning experiences are indexed in relation to learning complexity. Content and experiences numbered *1* are on the perceptual-motor level; those numbered *2* are on the perceptual level; and those numbered *3* are on the associative-conceptual level. There may be any number of content factors and experiences on each level. The following is an example of content on level 1 and some related experiences on three levels for kindergarten instruction.

The basic idea to be learned is that there are many kinds of animals. The content of the lesson is (1.0) animals move in different ways, they walk, crawl, fly, or swim. Learning experiences related to content follow:

Level *1*. Motor-balance posture. Have children (1) stand like animals on four legs, two legs, or one leg like cranes; (2) hang by hands and arms like monkeys; (3) lie on backs, stomachs, and sides.

Level *1*. Auditory-vocal recognition. Have children recognize sounds made by animals from (1) recordings; (2) teacher's imitation; and (3) imitation by other children.

Level *1*. Locomotion. Have children execute animal walks for stunts or creative activities: high stepping horse; crab walk (front, back, and sideways); elephant; frog; worm; bear; lame puppy walk; kitten (arched back); crow (hands on ankles); and camel walk (hands clasped over back, with chin moving in and out).

Level *1*. Let children construct scenes of barnyard or circus using toy animals. Teach for concepts: over-under, away-near, right-left, little-big. Order relationships, when more than two degrees of variation exist: large-largest, small-smallest, right-near right, left-near left.

Level *2*. Dramatize, *What Am I?* Children make a choice of an animal to tell about while others guess. Teacher starts by being the first animal, e.g. "I am tall. I sometimes have one or two humps. You will find me in deserts. People ride on me. I can go without water for a long time."

Level 3. Have children classify pictures of animals on the bulletin board under the headings: Walking Animals; Crawling Animals; Flying Animals; Swimming Animals. Personal scrapbook could also be made. In addition to classifying animals by locomotion they could group them by beginning letter name, color, size, wild-tame, fur-feathers, skin-scales, and so forth.

At the beginning of the school year the teacher may need to start all of the children in level 1 activities and let them progress at their own rate. As she secures data on each child she then can make more definite assignments. Instruments such as the Purdue Perceptual-Motor Survey, The Illinois Test of Psycholinguistic Abilities, The Frostig Development Test of Visual Perception and Spraing's Behavior Rating Scale could be used to great advantage to acquire relevant information for making level assignments and determining appropriateness of activities.

Some children may have to start at level I while others may start with activities at level 2 or 3. All the children would eventually be engaged in one of the three levels with different activities, methods, and materials but all working on common curricular objectives. Three areas within the room could serve as level centers for group and individual work, storage of materials, and so on. With a property administered program, there would be no more stigma attached to the level centers than that which now exists in reading or mathematics groups. The status of some children may not permit them to progress beyond level 1 or 2; however, the groupings should be flexible so that each child has the opportunity to work out of one area and into the next higher level.

Much attention has been given to patterns of organization for instruction and for restructuring of the curriculum and its content. More recently, models for instruction have been advanced that pertain to the teacher's role in the teaching-learning process. Another critical step must be taken in this chain of progression. We must seek ways to help the classroom teacher impart the information necessary for establishing transferable critical thinking and behavior patterns. One way to do this is to secure the best fit between materials, methods, and the child's manner of accommodating and assimilating stimuli. The child's classroom activities should be structured to build conceptual frameworks rather than to develop splintered skills or nonintegrated experiences.

In our efforts to maximize the cognitive status of the child we do not minimize the importance of his emotional life. The child who has more successful experiences is more likely to feel adequate and interact positively in his physical and social world.

REFERENCES

1. Dunsing, J. D., and Kephart, N. C.: Motor generalizations in space and time. In J. Hellmuth (Ed.): *Learning Disorders*, Seattle, Special Child, 1965, Vol. 1.
2. Karplus, Robert, *et al.*: *Relativity of Position and Motion*. Science Improvement Study. Berkeley, Univ. California, 1964.
3. Kephart, Newell C.: *The Slow Learner in the Classroom*. Columbus, C. E. Merrill, 1960.
4. Kephart, Newell C.: Perceptual-motor aspects of learning disabilities. *Excep Child*, 31:4, December 1964.
5. Peter, L.: *Prescriptive Teaching*. New York, McGraw-Hill, 1965.
6. Piaget, J.: *The Origins of Intelligence in Children*. Internat. Univ. Press, 1952.
7. Russell, David H.: *Children's Thinking*. Boston, Ginn, 1956.
8. Spraings, Violet: *Implications of Psychologic Testing for the Detection and Education of Neurologically Handicapped Children*. Pleasant Hill, Calif., Contra Costa County Dept. of Education, 1963.
9. Taba, Hilda: *Curriculum Development Theory and Practice*. New York, Harcourt, Brace and World, 1962.
10. Taba, Hilda, and Hills, Janies L.: *Teacher Handbook for Contra Costa Social Studies Grades 1-6*. Hayward, Calif., Rapid Printers and Lithographers, 1965.

Chapter 18

SUGGESTED ENVIRONMENT AND SOME BASIC PHILOSOPHY FOR A CLASS FOR EDUCATIONALLY HANDICAPPED CHILDREN

MADELEINE LASSERS

PART I ENVIRONMENT

Classroom

CONSIDERED IDEAL in the present project is a room large enough to seat children well apart and to have different activities going on without interferring with each other, i.e. a room considered large enough for the average group of thirty is about right for eight neurologically handicapped children.

Provision should be made for cutting down the space for individual children and activities in order to avoid the feeling of "floating off" in space. Large, stable, movable partitions, plus three-sided "private offices" for each child's desk are ideal. Windows should be blocked off by paint or some other means of cutting out outdoor distractions while admitting the light.

Furnishings

Besides the partitions, small individual tables for desks and a small shelf of some sort should be provided for each child. Tables which can be fitted together to form a large table would be most ideal. Tables should be approximately 36 × 24 inches with adjustable height. Two or three large tables for lunch and other activities are needed, plus chairs, book shelves and *closed* cupboard space for all materials. Space for storing each child's

Reprinted from the *Journal Of The California Optometric Association*, January, 1966, pp. 34-41. By permission of the author and publisher.

work and materials away from his office is needed. He then takes only one or two work assignments to his office at a time. This helps him stick at one job until it is finished and avoids the distraction of other materials. It also provides him with a structured need to move about ever so often and tends to minimize aimless wandering resulting from the difficulty he is apt to have in staying in one place for very long.

Maps, a globe, reference and "fun" books, along with some of the work of the children may be arranged or displayed in a corner behind two or more of the partitions. Individual children may use these materials as they need them, or as they are able to tolerate the added stimulation. Single maps may be displayed on the inside of a partition and the partition pulled out to expose the one map as it is needed.

A bulletin board in the school hall where work or projects may be displayed is excellent. Probably the only materials which should be on general display in the room are a clock and a flag, and for some groups these may be too distracting at the beginning. The teacher's desk should have little on it and when working with a child only the materials actually being used should be displayed. A closed mobile cart where the teacher can place materials she will use for the day which she can push around from desk to desk or table to table is excellent. One or two easels with paint, and so forth, may be kept up but placed so that they are out of the view of children not using them.

Class Size

Eight children are about as many as one full-time teacher and a part-time helper can handle.

Recess

Provisions for limiting and structuring recesses should be made. Gradually increasing participation in general recesses involving large groups and "free play" may come as the children improve in self-control.

Teachers

Teachers of these classes are subject to far more than the usual amount of frustration and tension. A vast amount of preparation for each individual child is needed, often involving making the materials used. Provision should be made for help (typing), in this work and some arrangement should be made which allows *time* for this preparation. The teacher needs understanding and support from her administrators.

New Classes

New classes are best started with one or two children, the others to be added as the first ones become accustomed to the routine. "Make haste slowly" is a wise admonition for these groups. Where at all possible, consideration might be given to a "staggered arrival and departure" of children daily, with a few in the morning, all there in the middle of the day, and the late comers making a small group in the afternoon.

Rest

If children are present for a full-day some provision for resting, perhaps on cots, is advisable. Their very hyperactivity and tension wears them out without their realizing it.

Parent-Teacher Conferences

Parent-teacher conferences are very important. A good understanding of what the teacher and school are trying to do for the child and how they hope to accomplish their goals tends to create confidence and cooperation on the part of the parents. Again this takes more than the usual amount of time on the teacher's part and should be taken into consideration.

Visitors

Visitors cannot be tolerated by NH groups. One visit and most of a day's work is lost. Observation should be through a one-way screen only.

Length of Stay in Class

The learning problems, personality and behavior difficulties exhibited by most of these children cannot be helped in a brief time. Most of them *can* be helped, but it is a long, slow process involving many subtle changes. It seems to this teacher that a child who is ready to return to a regular class in a year's time didn't really need to come into the class, but rather needed some remedial work.

PART II BASIC PHILOSOPHY

Certain behavior problems seem characteristic of a large number of neurologically handicapped children. The following are some of the problems and the ways in which we have attempted to meet them.

Problem 1

Most of these children are unable to screen out any stimuli and are thus bombarded by distracting stimuli from every direction.

MEETING THE PROBLEM. We attempt to control this by making the schoolroom as free of general stimuli as possible and exposing the child to the *one* stimulus we wish him to attend to. This is done by blocking out the windows or using a black paper screen over a book with "windows" cut in it so as to expose one line or one word at a time. The teacher dresses simply with no distracting patterns in her clothes, no earrings, beads, flowers, or exciting colors.

Problem 2

Most of these children are highly distractable and many are hyperactive to an extreme degree.

MEETING THE PROBLEM. Everything possible is done to cut out distractions. Each child works alone in his office or alone with the teacher at her desk or a table with a screen to cut off any movement of the other children. The classroom atmosphere is relaxed and extremely quiet with an emphasis on not doing anything to disturb the other workers. (Some provision for occasional *nonpunitive* exclusion from the group needs to be made.) As children improve in self-control and ability to concentrate they are encouraged to move their desks out in the room, whenever they are able to work there.

At the beginning of our class all work was individual, one child at a time with the teacher and *no* group work. First attempt at group activities in the last half hour of the day resulted in bedlam; it was given up and several weeks later started again, first bringing two children together on part of a project, then another two on another part of the same project. When these two groups were going well they were joined in a continuation of the same project and another group of two started. By the end of the first year, five or six of the children were able to work on a joint project, coming together briefly and then separating in two's or three's to carry on. By the end of the second year, afternoons could be pretty well devoted to group projects with usually one or sometimes two children needing to work in the "peace and quiet" (the phrase is that of one of the children) of his own office. Morning academic work is still mostly one child with the teacher, though two and sometimes three children may work together in some areas. They are often paired not on a quality of achievement basis but on a supplementary basis. A child who reads well but does not always understand what he reads works with a child who reads not as well but understands easily.

Problem 3

Most of these children are disorganized, unable to make choices, can't decide where to start or when to stop.

MEETING THE PROBLEM. The program is highly structured and few (at first, no) opportunities for choices are offered. Each child knows exactly what he is to do when he comes in in the morning and every attempt is made to see that he carries through on every job. A highly structured program helps these children by eliminating the need to make decisions; eliminating much distraction, and helping them learn to organize their thoughts, work, and behavior. At the same time considerable flexibility is needed in order to adjust the program to the changing needs of individual children. By the end of the second year, children were being encouraged to *make* choices in certain limited areas.

Problem 4

Most of these children have experienced nothing but failure in the school situation and often failure in the home and social situation.

MEETING THE PROBLEM. Every child must have success every day. Only as he is able to tolerate it, is real criticism offered. Work tasks are such that the teacher *knows* he can experience success in at least some of the work. At first he must have success in almost everything he attempts. As he begins to see himself as a worthwhile individual with some capacities his work is gradually increased in difficulty. It may take many months before a child is working at his actual capacity where failure mingles with success. Even then correction is usually made by leading the child himself to find his error and correct it so he still achieves success. We work through strengths; first emphasizing what the child does best and only later working on his weakest areas.

Problem 5

Most of these children feel they are unsatisfactory. They are unhappy and unhappy about themselves. Many will explain their problem at great length. Many are highly inconsistent in performance. A child able to spell ten words today may remember only two of them three days later and again know them all the day after! A child working easily at third grade arithmetic may suddenly be unable to achieve at a first grade level! This characteristic occurred in a greater or less degree in all the children we worked with. In some, it was apparent often, but in fluctuating degrees. In some, it occurred only occasionally and at widely separated intervals.

MEETING THE PROBLEM. Remember this is going to pass and then return. The child who is suddenly frustrated by his inability to do the work he has been doing with a real sense of accomplishment is told, "Let's put this away for awhile and try this, it will help you understand your regular work better," and something *different*, not just easier, is substituted. If you find it is an "off" day for a child, change his assignments for the day or several days or weeks, as needed. Basic to the child's academic achievement or behavior improvement is his feeling about himself and his relationship with the teacher. Once he comes to feel that she is "on his side," is his friend who has some understanding of his difficulties and wants to help him, he wants (most of the time) to *work* with her. Once he begins to feel he is a worthwhile person who can do *some* desirable things he is ready to go. The teacher needs *to achieve a gentle but absolute* firmness and avoid being against the child. If possible, never catch him doing something he shouldn't do. Give some kind of warning that will stop him *before* he realizes you are aware of his transgression. (This, of course, does not apply to some situations as one child hurting another.) *Anticipate* difficulties and start the child down a different path. Change his activity or his pace. Maybe the work is too hard, maybe there was some unhappy occurrence at home before he left. Often his posture at his desk will be a warning to you. *Frequently* his walk across the room tells you he's forgotten to take his pill, he's about to have a seizure, or he's looking for some outlet for unbearable frustrations. Many times you can help him *before* a situation arises by supplying him with an acceptable outlet for his frustrations.

Problem 6

Most of these children are disinhibited, lack self-control.

MEETING THE PROBLEM. Definite and positive limits need to be set and the teacher must know the child understands them, but these limits need to be broad and basic, not picayune and constricting. In the case of the experimental class they were simple, "You may not hurt anyone else. You may not destroy anyone else's or the school's property. You must behave so that other people who want to work may do so."

In our group *verbal* attack was entirely acceptable toward the teacher but not toward the other children. When uncomplimentary remarks or appelations are addressed to other children the addressee is apt to become upset and angry. Therefore, it was generally considered, through discussions of courtesy and kindness, bad form to call other children names. However, again in discussions, it was pointed out to the children that the teacher was a grown-up who understood much about their difficulty and knew they sometimes were angry, so if they called her names or said unkind things about her she understood why they did it. She was sorry they were angry but she was not mad at them. Every attempt was made to free children from any sense of guilt about such an outburst. Out of eight children, four exhibited this behavior, one even resorting to physical attack on the teacher (this was not tolerated). Within six months three of the four had passed through this phase, and at the end of the year the fourth no longer seemed to need this outlet.

CONCLUSION

The teacher of a neurologically handicapped group herself experiences considerably more than the usual amount of frustration. The very inconsistency of the children's performance can, at times, be bewildering. Their often unpredictable, disinhibited behavior can be exasperating for the minute, especially when she is annoyed, tired, or discouraged. However, it would seem that a mature adult with insight and considerable understanding of the difficulties these children experience, though at times she may purposely exhibit righteous indignation, cannot be truly exasperated with them. In our group when something exasperating occurs the teacher habitually closes her eyes, turns her head toward the ceiling, clasps her hands, and counts slowly and distinctly to ten. This is accepted as a sign that teacher is "holding on to herself" (something the children are frequently asked to do). Children stop and watch and laugh gently, since they understand it's a kind of a joke, and when the counting is done everyone sighs and returns to business as usual. When all else fails there is a desk available in an adjoining storeroom (with light and ventilation) where a noisy or uncontrolled child may work alone until able to be reasonably quiet in his own office. During the first month this was used frequently; by the end of the second year it was very rarely used. Final action involves the child's staying home for a day or two, not as punishment but simply to rest and "get hold" of himself. For this to be useful very careful preparatory work needs to be done with the parents. This final action was used several times for *one* child.

Many of our children have worked out rather intricate methods for controlling their environments. Scenes of various sorts, temper tantrums, tears, depressions, "I've given up—I'm a failure", violence toward members of families or teachers, all originally expressed extreme frustrations. All too often, however, the child soon learns that these activities on his part result in annoyance, anger, dismay, and sometimes actual fright on the part of the adults in his environment (not to mention his siblings).

Thus, the child's behavior becomes a "big stick" in his hands. A sort of "cold war" situation results with the child on one side and everyone else on the other side, and the "balance of power" frequently rests with the child! It is important for the child to learn more acceptable ways of behavior for his own sake and for the sake of his family's sanity! It is first necessary to find ways of circumventing as much of his frustration as possible, find things in which he *can* be successful and give him attention, praise, and recognition for his efforts toward desirable behavior. Undesirable behavior should receive as little attention as possible. If attempts to rechannel his activity and then mild reprovals do not bring desired results he should be excluded from the group and sent to his own room until he is able to control himself; then forget it; start anew; don't harp on poor behavior but *do* harp on desirable behavior. Do everything possible to build up his good feelings about himself, to help him find friends and interesting activities. A twelve-year-old boy once said to me, as we were discussing his misdeeds, "I have nothing to look forward to!" Help your child have "something to look forward to!" Plan interesting activities such as a fishing trip or a ball game with Dad, a family jaunt to the beach, a trip to the museum, any of a dozen of simple things—but schedule them—put them on your calendar so he can look forward to them.

Remember he is disinhibited,
uncontrolled,
hyperactive,
has perceptual difficulties which make the world most confusing
can't "screen out" any stimuli
has few or no friends
is a stranger to success
that the average environment is wildly exciting to him and causes him utter confusion.

Remember that patterns of behavior that have existed for years take years to change.

Remember, too, that he needs quiet, order, limits, *control* and love!

Chapter 19

THE SYSTEMATIC SELECTION
OF INSTRUCTIONAL MATERIALS
BASED ON AN INVENTORY OF
LEARNING ABILITIES AND SKILLS

JUDITH WEINTHALLER and JAY M. ROTHBERG

CONSIDERABLE ATTENTION has been focused on the availability and selection of materials for instructing the handicapped. Although substantial progress has been made in publicizing and disseminating these materials, little emphasis has been given to establishing a system for selecting materials according to particular learning abilities. Often, material is chosen at random from available catalogs or on the basis of a few children's needs rather than the diverse needs within a classroom. Selection often tends to be based solely on subject matter. This practice leads to either an overabundance or a lack of materials in a particular category, since one type of material cannot cover the complete range of learning abilities. In addition, how materials may be modified to teach various skills and how the presentation and response may be adapted to many different learning abilities are often not considered.

A system for selecting appropriate materials based on an inventory of learning abilities is described here. From such an analysis, the materials can be matched to the specific needs and abilities of the children who will use them.

The system will be discussed in two parts: its application to selecting and modifying materials for a particular child, and its use in choosing materials for groups of children with varying

Reprinted from *Exceptional Children*, Vol. 36 (1970), pp. 615-619. By permission of the senior author and publisher.

learning abilities. The selection procedure uses the same set of variables to analyze the learning abilities of a single child or a group of children and the type of problem for which the material is best suited.

SELECTING MATERIALS FOR INDIVIDUALS

With the heightened demand for instructional materials and their increased production and dissemination, education has often focused upon the material as the prime variable and first step in the teaching process. In working with handicapped children, however, the child's abilities should be evaluated first; only then can the appropriate materials be selected. The teaching process should begin with a determination of the learner's profile through a complete evaluation of his assets and deficits. From this profile, general remedial approaches should be determined, the teaching tasks specified, and the components placed in a logical developmental sequence beginning with the child's readiness and interest levels.

In addition to a learner's profile, a materials' profile, based on a similar analysis, should also be formulated. By comparing the two profiles, the best materials for each part of the teaching task can be selected, and the concept of diagnostic teaching (basing remediation on an initial and ongoing evaluation) can be effectively used.

Both of these profiles are compiled by using the six specific variables already employed in analyzing diagnostic and remedial learning tasks or activities: (1) level of the task, (2) modality of reception, (3) modality of expression, (4) types of psycholinguistic processes, (5) the number of modalities, and (6) the content of the task. These six variables are further explained by the following outline:

I. Level of the Task (according to a developmental hierachy of learning experiences)
   A. Sensation—most concrete, earliest, basic level of functioning
   B. Perception
   C. Memory
   D. Symbolization
   E. Conceptualization—most abstract, highest level of functioning

II. Modality of Reception (information is received through one or more of the following channels)
   A. Auditory
   B. Visual
   C. Tactile
III. Modality of Expression
   A. Auditory-oral (phonemes, words, environmental sounds)
   B. Motor-tactile-kinesthetic (gestures, pointing, marking, matching, drawing, writing)
IV. Psycholinguistic Processes
   A. Reception
   B. Association
   C. Expression
V. Number of Modalities (involved in the reception-association-expression sequence of a task)
   A. One modality—aural-oral (listening and speaking)
   B. Two modalities—aural-motor (listening and writing)
VI. Content of the Task (may be characterized by whether it is verbal or nonverbal and social or nonsocial)
   A. Verbal nonverbal content
      1. Verbal: involving both the auditory and visual modalities phonemes, letters, words, both oral and printed). The word *cat* either printed or head is considered verbal task content.
      2. Nonverbal: other means of communication and symbolization such as pictures, gestures, objects, environmental sounds, and numbers. A picture of a cat is nonverbal task content.
   B. Social nonsocial content
      1. Social: meaningful part of a child's environment such as environmental sounds and pictures.
      2. Nonsocial: nonmeaningful part of an environment such as pure tones, nonsense figures, nonsense syllables, or words.

Using the above variables, a profile of the learner's assets and deficits and a complementary materials profile is constructed, forming a Learner-Material Match. In a Learner-Material Match, the materials should capitalize upon the child's assets as well as strengthen his areas of weakness.

To illustrate an appropriate match, let us assume that a child has a deficit on the perceptual level, primarily in the auditory modality of reception and expression; in the visual modality, however, his abilities are relatively intact. In terms of task content his problem is verbal in nature. Let us also assume the teaching task is to strengthen the child's auditory discrimination. The material selected should not only involve an oral exchange, but also capitalize upon his visual strengths. Therefore, materials on the perceptual level should be selected which employ visual cues and motor gesture responses.

To illustrate an inappropriate Learner-Material Match, let us assume that a learner's profile consists of deficits in visual perception of verbal material and auditory strengths, while the materials' profile consists of nonverbal, nonsocial visual perceptual material (discrimination between meaningless designs) requiring visual motor responses. Although this material is on the correct hierarchy level, it is not appropriate for two reasons. First, its nonverbal and nonsocial task content is unrelated to the child's verbal problem; and second, it does not capitalize upon the child's auditory or tactile strengths. If the profiles are not matched, the instructional materials will probably not relate directly to the child's total learning needs. When both remediation and materials selection are not based on the diagnostic evaluation, the concept of diagnostic teaching is of little value.

SELECTING MATERIALS FOR GROUPS

The concept of a Learner-Material Match for individual children can also be applied to choosing materials for groups of children found, for example, in clinics, classrooms, and learning centers. Assuming that the individual profiles will vary, the first step is to establish a general framework of group learning abilities as a basis for selecting a master materials library. This collection must cover a wide range of learning abilities because the materials best suited for each child will be drawn from it. For example, in training two children with different auditory perceptual problems (one with strengths and one with deficiencies in visual perception and visual motor abilities) two types of materials are necessary: a type which capitalizes on the first child's visual perceptual strengths and another type which does not overemphasize visual input or visual motor response for the second child.

DISCUSSION OF LEARNING ABILITIES FRAMEWORK

The six variables used for individual diagnostic purposes form the basis for selecting the master collection and developing a general framework of learning abilities. The major headings in this framework are perception, memory, and symbolization-conceptualization—three of the five levels of the task hierarchy. Because remediation at the sensation level is more of a medical than educational concern, this level has not been included. The task levels of conceptualization and symbolization are combined because, although theoretically distinct, they are difficult to separate in the teaching process; both levels involve higher mental processes and require significantly more integration than the perceptual or memory levels.

Modalities of input are the subheadings and are followed by more specific breakdowns of learning abilities with specific suggestions for materials. Under the primary learning modalities of visual and audition, the additional variables of modality of expression and task content should be considered as often as possible.

Since the following outline of the learning abilities framework is merely a guide to a more efficient selection of materials based on a systematic inventory of learning abilities, little attempt has been made to include examples of all of the theoretically possible combinations of the six variables.

I. Perception
   A. Auditory Perception
      1. Gross discrimination
         a. Nonverbal: tapes, records, pictures, noisemakers, environmental sounds.
         b. Verbal: lists and pictures of dissimilar whole words having different initial, medial, and final sounds, i.e. banana-telephone, mailman-rosebud.
      2. Fine discrimination
         a. Nonverbal: sounds involving finer and more subtle discrimination—bells, animals, horns, footsteps, voices.
         b. Verbal: lists of morphemes and phonemes involving subtle discriminations—money-monkey, men-mend, fine-vine, house-mouse, bell-ball, s-d, s-c, d-b—phonics cards, and games.

B. Visual perception
  1. Discrimination
      a. Form and shape discrimination
          (1) Nonverbal: two and three dimensional objects, numbers, geometric forms, shape and number templates and inserts, peg boards.
          (2) Verbal: two and three dimensional letters, letter stencils, templates, tactile letters, and block words (discrimination of word configurations).
      b. Color discrimination: objects and cards for matching, sorting, pasting.
      c. Size discrimination
          (1) Nonverbal: graduated cylinders, nesting boxes, three dimensional numbers.
          (2) Verbal: two and three dimensional letters and words varying in height and length.
  2. Constancy
      a. Nonverbal: objects, pictures, numbers varying in size, shape, position of viewing, color, and texture.
      b. Verbal: letters, words, sentences varying in size, shape, position, color, context, and texture; visual tracking of letters and words; varying styles of letters and anagrams; words printed on paper of varying colors.
  3. Part-whole relationship
      a. Nonverbal: form puzzles, single figure and picture puzzles, toys and objects to construct and assemble, fraction insert puzzles, cuisinaire rods, parquetry blocks, balance scale, abacus.
      b. Verbal: letter puzzles, letters to cut up, word builders (linking letters), sentence builders, syllabication lists and cards.
  4. Figure ground
      a. Nonverbal: objects for sorting, hidden figure pictures, picture tracking exercise.
      b. Verbal: symbol and word tracking exercises, hidden letter and word exercises, reading frames.
  5. Visual motor
      a. Fine motor: stencils, templates, construction toys, arts and crafts activities, programed handwriting exercise books, bean bag and ring toss games, jacks, paints, throwing and catching games, nuts and bolts, acetate overlays, grease pencils, writing frames, corrective pencils, daily living materials such as buttons, zippers, ties, and eating utensils.

      b. Gross motor: records for body movement development, trampoline, walking boards, climbing ropes and bars, barrels, balance boards, medicine ball, staircase, and other playground equipment.

  C. Body perception (laterality, body image, body schema)—dolls, pictures of humans, people puzzles, manikin, mirror, balance board, trampoline, walking board, videotapes, polaroid cameras, film strips, records for developing body image

  D. Temporal perception—real clocks and calendars, teaching clocks and calendars, pictures to emphasize significant events and seasons, stories involving temporal sequences of events, rhythm instruments and activities, materials for estimation of temporal duration such as a timer and a stopwatch, and equipment for pouring liquids and drawing to music

  E. Social perception—pictures portraying various facial expressions and emotions, cause-effect pictures, picture interpretation activities, group games

II. Memory

  A. Auditory

    1. Recall—pictures to aid recall of auditory commands and sentence repetition; art projects and games for following directions; games stressing auditory recall; objects and pictures for rapid naming

    2. Sequencing

      a. Nonverbal: tapes with sequences of environmental sounds and instrumental sounds using real objects and pictures to accompany tapes; buzzer boards; and pattern cards.

      b. Verbal: picture cards and word lists for training sequences of initial, medial, and final sounds and auditory blending of sounds; letters and cards to reinforce the recall of sequences of sounds and words; programed exercises for audio-visual equipment; dual track tape recorders.

  B. Visual

    1. Recall—objects, pictures, numbers, words, and letters to be recalled; flash cards, programed worksheets, tachistoscope or tachistoscopic attachment for overhead projectors

    2. Sequencing

      a. Nonverbal: beads for stringing, numbers for sequencing, different shaped blocks and designs.

      b. Verbal: manipulative block letters for imitation of sequential patterns, exercises for matching letter sequences.

III. Symbolization-conceptualization
    A. Oral language (verbal symbols)
        1. Reception (listening)—materials geared to teaching nouns, parts of speech, sentence structure, and concepts or categories not requiring a spoken response to confirm the child's understanding of the information presented; real objects for manipulation; pictorial representations of nouns, verbs, adjectives, and prepositions; film strips, lotto games, language development kits, stories to be read
        2. Expression (speaking)—walkie talkie sets, tape recorder, dual track tape recorder, phonics mirror, large action pictures, hand and finger puppets, stimulation cards
    B. Written language (verbal)
        1. Reception (reading)—reading materials using whole, phonetic, linguistic, and tactile-kinesthetic methods; reading clinics; exercises for reading comprehension, concept and vocabulary building, and following directions; independent high interest, low vocabulary reading
        2. Expression (writing)—learning abilities not involving visual motor coordination, but including spelling, sentence formulation, production, and level of ideation
           a. Programed spelling workbooks, sentence building cards, tape recorders, and picture sequences to increase written productivity.
           b. Typewriters, letter charts, wide lined paper, letter stamp sets (aids which should be provided since this category does not deal with visual motor coordination).
    C. Arithmetic (nonverbal symbols)—number lines, stepping stones, counting objects, boxes, frames, ladders, abacus, flash cards, place value charts, fraction boards, programed workbooks, real and play money, number charts, and stamp sets

SUMMARY

Failure to establish a systematic framework of learning abilities often results in a random selection of instructional materials based on factors such as availability of catalogs, learning profiles of a limited number of children, or subject matter alone. This type of selection rarely relates to the child's needs and abilities. Without the appropriate materials, the remedial teaching process is impeded. Only by establishing such a sytematic framework can materials be selected to insure a Learner-Material Match and, therefore, to insure the full application of the concept of diagnostic teaching.

Chapter 20

A LESSON PLAN FOR
EDUCATIONALLY HANDICAPPED CHILDREN
IN LEARNING DISABILITY GROUPS

R. G. HECKELMAN

LEARNING DISABILITY GROUPS are one of the ways neurologically handicapped children can be educated in California schools. Group class sizes are limited to eight students under certain conditions of age span. The following describes one program which has had success.

The learning situation was structured from the beginning to use conditioning processes. Creativity and extreme permissiveness were not encouraged. Students were urged to be learning actively every minute. The teacher created a classroom atmosphere that was warm, structured, and positive. Little time was spent on correction of mistakes, as the work was arranged so that most of the activity of the child was correct and progressed from one small success to another. Children were not encouraged to read or write on their own in class; pencils were not allowed to be put to paper until training assured successful motor movement of the child.

The Neurological Impress Method[4] was used in various forms throughout the training.

Although creating new teaching materials is important, it is also important not to forget methods which have proved successful in an effort to be creative. Many of the teaching activities here have been borrowed and adapted liberally from the pub-

Reprinted from the *Academic Therapy Quarterly*, Vol. 2 (1966), pp. 18-22. By permission of the author and publisher.

lished works of Fernald,[2] Cruikshank,[1] Kephart,[5] Getman,[3] and others.

The following lesson plans are only a segment of the total program and are not meant to be repeated in every segment each day. They do help answer the question of beginning teachers in the field of the educationally handicapped, "How do you teach these children?"

Mrs. Ruth Erlandson of Elim Elementary School, Hilmar Unified School District, Hilmar, California, who had previously taught only in the regular classroom, undertook to work with the author in developing a program for these handicapped children.

Mrs. Erlandson met with three learning disability groups each day. The first was a primary group of six children. All groups met for one and a half hours daily. The second group was of fourth graders, the third group fifth and sixth graders.

On the following pages is a suggested lesson plan for one day. The time allotted to specific materials is listed on the left. Following this, another lesson plan, given for purposes of variation, is described in the same manner.

A spot check of the students in the program indicated a gain averaging five months of learned reading in three months. This is compared to previous gains of less than one month for each month in the regular classroom. All children in the program had learning disabilities in excess of two years of their expectancy levels. This gain was made in spite of a classroom move to smaller, more inadequate quarters caused by a fire in one of the schools which destroyed several classrooms.

1. *10 minutes*

    Use comic strip "Peanuts"
    or "Dennis the Menace."

    Project on screen with
    opaque projector.

    A. Children read aloud with
    teacher, following pointer,
    as often as needed.

    B. Child reads individually if
    success is assured, following
    teacher's sliding pointer.

2. *10 minutes*

    Project typed phrases from a
    story to be used later.

    "He would not listen," from
    Just for Fun

    A. Projected phrases preread by
    teacher, repeated several
    times.
    1. a little hen
    2. would not listen
    3. many strawberries
    4. wait a day

3. *10 minutes*

    Relaxation time.
    Talk to children about a
    current interest.
    Overhead projector.

    A. Using the overhead projector
    write down some of their sen-
    tences as they are talking.
    Avoid question-and-answer
    teaching technique.

    B. Example of one day's conversa-
    tion:
    1. "Yesterday my horse had a
    colt."
    2. "I have a horse named
    Rocky."
    3. "Everyday I ride my horse."
    4. "My horse is brown and
    white."

    C. Children watch teacher write
    and say it. It is read together
    in unison. Opportunity is
    allowed for individual reading.

4. *15 minutes*

    Use of pegboards.
    Each child has a 100 hole
    pegboard with colored pegs.
    A duplicate of their board is
    made on paper.

    A. Making pegboard designs.
    1. A simple design using two
    or three colors is made on the
    paper. The children make
    the same design on their
    boards using the same
    colors and putting them in
    the exact spaces.

Example:

```
                                              blue
          .                        .  .  .  .  .  .  .  .  .
       .    .                                           .
                                                      .
     .        .                                     .
                                                  .
   .          .                                 .
                      blue                    .
 red     .      .                           .
                                          .          red
     .          .                       .
                                      .
   .              .                  .
                                   .
 .                  .            .
 .  .  .  .  .  .  .  .    .  .  .  .  .  .  .  .  .  .
       green                       blue
```

5. 10 minutes
Reading systems readiness.

From Continental Press, Reading Fundamental Program packets, *Independent Activities—Level 2*

A. Children trace over the design with their finger a number of times. The design is then retraced numerous times with a pencil. The third step is to draw the design free hand. (Later the design may be drawn from memory.)

6. 15 minutes
Blackboard work.
Use of fiberboard templates. Large, medium, and small templates, square, triangle and other geometric designs, also patterns (developed by Heckelman) patterned after writing motor patterns.

A. Traced in the same manner as the paper work. Trace repeatedly with the finger, then chalk, remove the template and trace with chalk over the design they have copied, erase design and draw freehand if degree of success is reasonably assured.

7. 15 minutes
Tape recorder—individual earphones.

Story from *Just for Fun*

A. The story, *Just for Fun*, is prerecorded by teacher, children listen to the story as read by the teacher as they follow the story in their books. The tape is then repeated and the children read aloud with the tape using their books.

(note) Markers are used by each child to show that he is following correctly; pictures in the book are blacked out.

Lesson Plan for Another Day

1. *10 minutes*
   Comic strip, "Nancy" and
   "Priscilla's Pop."
   Project on opaque projector.

   A. Use in same manner as first
      lesson plan 1.

2. *10 minutes*
   Discuss favorite games with
   children. Use overhead projector and transparencies.

   A. Write what children tell on
      overhead projector transparency
      1. "My brothers and I like to
         play football."
      2. "Yesterday I hit the baseball
         and made a home run."
      3. "I like to swim in a canal."

3. *15 minutes*
   a 2 × 4 inch × 15 foot board

   A. First walk forward, then back-
      ward, then sideways. Walk
      with arms free. Then walk
      holding a stick with both
      hands.

4. *5 minutes*
   Rhythm Record
   Record Phoebe James—
   frog, rabbit, airplane

   A. Skip, jump, and hop as
      directed.

5. *5 minutes*
   Rubber ball

   A. Listen for rhythm pattern as
      teacher bounces ball. Both
      eyes closed and opened.

   B. Have children listen for certain
      number of bounces, then have
      them repeat exactly.

6. *15 minutes*
   Picture study.

   Either opaque, overhead projector or filmstrip.

   A. Have children study picture and
      ask them to tell everything
      they can remember about it.

   B. Then ask specific questions
      such as:
      1. What colors did you see?
      2. What animals? (if any)
      3. What was the biggest object
         in the picture?
      4. What was in the lower,
         right hand corner?
      5. What was at the top?
      6. What shapes did you see?

   C. Project the picture again
      and review the questions.

7. *15 minutes*
   Listening for directions.
   Microphone, amplifier,
   earphones.
   Teacher gives directions orally
   over the microphone to the
   children who are wearing earphones.

   A. "Johnny, walk to the door,
   touch the floor with your right
   hand, come back and sit down."
   "Danny, go to the board, get
   a piece of chalk and give it to
   Jimmy."
   "Carl, walk backwards to the
   window, turn around three
   times and come back to your
   seat walking backwards."

8. *20 minutes*
   Tape recorder and
   listening post.

   Teacher reads phrases from
   a story which has been typed
   on paper and numbered.

   A. Let each child read a phrase
   into the microphone for the
   others to hear

   Call out a number and have
   someone read the correct
   phrases, or read a phrase
   and ask the child to reply if he
   has the right number.

   B. Review story from previous day.
   C. Have the children read along
   with the prerecorded story on
   the tape recorder.

REFERENCES

1. Cruikshank, Wm. M., Bentzen, Frances A., Tatzeburg, Frederick M., and Tannhauser, Marian T.: *A Teaching Method for Brain-Injured and Hyperactive Children.* New York, Syracuse Univ., 1961.
2. Fernald, Grace M.: *Remedial Techniques in Basic School Subjects.* New York, McGraw-Hill, 1943.
3. Getman, G. N., and Kane, Elmer R.: *The Physiology of Readiness.* Ed.D. Minneapolis, P.A.S.S., 1964.
4. Heckelman, R. G.: Using the neurological impress remedial reading technique. *Academic Therapy Q, 1:4,* 235-239, Summer, 1966.
5. Kephart, Newell C.: *The Slow Learner in the Classroom.* Columbus, O. C. E. Merrill, 1960.

Chapter 21

STRUCTURING A SPECIAL CLASS FOR THE NEUROLOGICALLY HANDICAPPED CHILD

GORDON H. NAYLOR

T HERE IS LARGE GROUP of handicapped children in our society who are in desperate need of adequate help. Little understood, they are seldom the object of sympathy, more often the object of ridicule and open rejection on the part of peers, parents, and teachers. These children are the neurologically handicapped (here referred to as NH) or the "brain-injured." The NH condition, like so many other handicaps, should be the subject of a rehabilitative program; one that will provide society with valuable persons capable of taking their places among the contributing citizenry.

Characteristically, the behavior of the neurologically handicapped child may be described as showing distractability, hyperactivity, hyperkinesity, disinhibition, and bizarreness. As one can see from this description of the NH child, many of his characteristics presuppose learning difficulties. This is a child who is abnormally responsive to the stimuli of his environment, who is highly distractable, who tends to respond in a disorganized way, who is conditioned to failure, and who cannot tolerate frustration. Thus when the NH child is faced with the necessity to synthesize (separate elements into integrated and meaningful wholes), conceptualize (project relationships in a logical sequence), or adapt a given skill to a new situation, he may be so overwhelmed by the task that he responds catastrophically. He blows up.

Reprinted from the *Journal Of The California Optometric Association*, January, 1966, pp. 11-15. By permission of the author and publisher.

The rehabilitative program for the NH child should be primarily an educational one, geared to the development of each child to his fullest potential. To help him, special facilities, special techniques and methods, and specially trained teachers of creative and resourceful ability are needed. Effective principles of instruction must be adapted to meet his unique and multifarious needs.

1. *Distractions should be kept at a minimum.* Since the NH child responds to any and all details, external stimuli are kept at a minimum by simplifying the environment. Walls and ceilings should be painted the same neutral color as the floor. There should be no pictures, bulletin board displays, pencil sharpeners, open shelves of books until he demonstrates the ability to work in such an environment without undue handicap. A self-contained room with toilets, drinking water, and freedom from visitors and interruptions is important. Teachers' dress should avoid jewelry and bright or checked colors. Children may be asked to wear plain and uniform colors such as white shirt and jeans.

2. *Isolation from other children is essential as a means of reducing distraction as well as relieving peer pressure until a sufficient level of tolerance for both is indicated.* As space is decreased, security is increased. The NH child should work alone in a cubicle on any task requiring sustained attention. Partitions keep children from seeing each other and decrease distracting noises. Desks fixed to the floor and facing the wall prevent excessive motor activity and distraction. Glass windows should be "one-way vision" to prevent the child from looking out.

3. *A therapeutic environment among a small group (six to eight) seems to effect the best relationships.* The classroom should be arranged to provide a life space that is stable and represents security for the child; one in which he can gain a mastery over his environment and predict the outcome of his actions. As this miniature world becomes more understandable to him he can develop a workable approach to reality that will carry over to everyday life.

4. *A highly structured program* where, with routine, the day's events can be predicted, will allow the child to relax and apply

attention to learning tasks. The class must be *teacher-structured* and *teached-dominated*. Unexpected changes or complex situations requiring perceptual reorganization of one's response, the generalization of similarities to unique situations, and the careful distinguishing of differences between things which appear similar, present an almost insurmountable condition to successful achievement for the NH child. To allow the NH child to make a choice when he is unable to respond selectively to his environment only produces tension and reinforces the child's sense of failure.

5. *Learning experiences should be so primitive that success is inevitable.* These children have not known success in school, their only experiences were those of reprimand and censorship. If the child's lesson is structured to the point where he is allowed only to do it the right way, the teacher can say "good," and the child will find satisfaction and develop confidence in his learning ability.

6. *Discipline must be firm and teacher-oriented.* The disorganized child finds direction and stability in a controlled envionment. Much disturbance can be prevented by planning ahead in a way that will avoid frustrating conditions. The child who appears insecure or breaks down to confused and erratic behavior following unexpected changes may require a detailed explanation of an event before its occurrence. This should include an attempt to anticipate specifically what the child is likely to experience, what he will be expected to say, why this event is happening, and how the adults feel about it. It is hoped that from a controlled environment the child will learn and internalize a system of controls.

7. *Instruction must be individualized to meet the needs of each child.* For the NH child, every lesson must be successfully begun and ended within the child's attention span. The tasks should be so simplified that they can be successfully completed. This requires unique lesson planning since a child may be achieving at the fourth grade level in arithmetic, the second in spelling, and experiencing little if any success in reading as a result of his handicap. Methods must be used that account for deficiencies both in abilities and in sensory perception.

8. *Learning should involve more than one perceptual field.* Teaching methods generally depend upon visual perception. Since this is often the most seriously damaged skill for the NH child, successful teaching makes it necessary to take advantage of the tactual, kinesthetic, and auditory learning abilities. Lessons can be spoken, written, acted out, and illustrated in an effort to compensate for the impaired perception. The use of color, where possible, is advisable since color perception is usually intact. Words written on sandpaper can be touched for clearer meaning, or might be written in sand or in clay.

9. *All learning should be accomplished with insight.* Insightful learning experiences for the NH child are extremely difficult to plan, in part because of the nature of the child's perceptual dysfunction. Insight requires that one be able to integrate each small part of the whole that is being taught into a broad generalized concept which gives a new understanding. Individual assignments must be made in small units, with well integrated relationships clearly defined, if the child is to retain the insightful experience so difficult for him to learn.

10. *Much use can be made of motor activities.* The NH child seems to be attracted by moving stimuli, and attention is often more readily obtained in this way. The use of concrete materials is needed where the more abstract abilities are impaired. There often exists a discrepancy between the ease with which an NH child deals with his object word and the picture world. Provisions for these slow transitions need to be made in the classrooms. The child may first use objects such as blocks to build structures according to a picture copy, or he may place pegs in a board according to a given pattern. As he learns to use pictures, he learns to perceive differences among them. This is a step toward future generalization.

11. *The use of drill* should be used on the problem process rather than on the answer. Habituation through drill only encourages verbalization. Many NH children possess an unusual facility for verbalization and the "parroting" of words without any real understanding.

12. *Activities should be varied to prevent meaningless perseveration.* (The NH child "perseverates" when he continues

repeating an activity, once begun, long after it has ceased to have any meaning or purpose.) Because of the security that comes with perseverating in a rigid and familiar course of action, perseveration becomes a common tendency with the NH child. The transition from one learning task to the next is thwarted by such meaningless, but comforting perseveration. One hazard is the tendency of the NH child to perseverate in an error. It is very important for him to be shown how the error can be corrected and not wait for additional experience to supply the organization which normally would make possible a spontaneous correction.

13. *Lessons should be carefully structured to the child's needs.* Where there is limited attention span there should be many short lessons rather than one long one. If impairment in one area hinders understanding, advantage of other perceptual areas should be taken. Creative materials and unique methods are needed for each child. No two will be impaired in the same areas or equal in ability and achievement levels. Most conventional curriculum materials and techniques will prove inadequate for the NH child. As an example, cursive writing should be taught rather than manuscript as a means of preventing rigidity in motor activity. Such a method emphasizes the wholeness of words, something needed due to the tendency of the NH child to dwell on parts and detail.

14. *As the child matures, every effort should be made to foster the process of generalization* as a basis for the development of concepts. The categorization of the particular, concrete objects of a situation into general classes is perhaps the most important of his learning mechanisms in the acquisition of cultural symbols. Categorization is according to function and use. Thus the ability to discern similarities under perceptual variations is required. This is accomplished by having the child sort pictures or classify words, first according to one principle and then another, always leading to a higher level of comparison.

The NH child tends to respond to details due to an inability to organize larger wholes based upon the similarity between two objects. The introduction of a new stimulus produces a state of imbalance which causes the child to seek relief by seizing upon the first detail he can identify. As a result, the irrelevant detail is often accepted as a substitute for that which is significant. The characteristic weakness of the NH child, then, is his tendency to specificity of concepts and narrow classifications. His boundaries are so narrow any reorganization of material into a more generalized nature is prevented.

15. *Much effort should be given to establishing a warm and secure working relationship with each child.* The teacher of NH children must be prepared for emotional blowups. At times the teacher has to physically restrain a child to prevent him from harming himself or others. If the child's arms are pinned to his side until he gains control, he discovers security in the physical strength of the teacher. Every time a child loses control, he also becomes more fearful. This is the time to stop the work and begin something new, often with the entire group.

The NH child greatly needs affection. This can be a way of rewarding worthy behavior. Also, as the child matures, there is an increase in his social awareness and his desire to be like other children, providing an incentive for him to learn to behave as others.

16. *The class should be carefully structured at the beginning of the year.* Each child should be accepted individually until a proper relationship is established (approximately five days) and then returned home while the next is oriented to the program. This also provides a time for individual appraisal and an evaluation of ability and achievement for the purpose of selecting materials. The child must know what is expected of him each moment of the day. Limits on behavior are carefully and firmly established. Routine is essential and the class must be so simple that there is a minimum of frustration.

The NH child who senses his difference and is aware of his learning difficulties will gladly accept arrangements which are planned to help him learn more effectively. He is eager to be accepted by others and delighted with the satisfaction that comes from being able to exert some control over his environment.

SECTION H

PARENT COUNSELING

Chapter 22

COUNSELING THE PARENT OF THE BRAIN-INJURED CHILD

Ray H. Barsch

T HE CHILD WITH BRAIN DAMAGE is a complex organism. While some progress has been made in understanding the complexity of this problem, investigative efforts have been largely centered on differentiating this child from others by means of psychological tests or upon his unique learning problems. This child has often been studied out of context. He is a social being and a full understanding of his problem is dependent upon viewing him in his social setting as well as in his test experiences.

The concern of his parents is great. They require as much help as their child. These parents are no less obligated to society than the parents of a normal child to transmit the culture and help the child become a sufficiently acceptable member of his social group so that he may survive socially as well as biologically.

Unfortunately, the parents of the brain-damaged child have been neglected in most research studies to date. The only significant effort in this particular field has been the publication of *The Other Child*, a small book for parents and laymen.[1]

Too many professional specialists give parents the feeling that they have little time to discuss the problems with them, communicate in a technical jargon that effectively confuses and overwhelms the parents, and generally show little or no interest in the personal problems of the parents.

Those who work with the parents should be able to vicariously experience the strength and nature of their frustrations while at

Reprinted from the *Journal Of Rehabilitation*, Vol. 27 (1961), pp. 1-3. By permission of the author and publisher.

the same time structuring the relationship so as to facilitate change in parent attitudes and practice. If we feel an obligation to the exceptional child, it is hard to justify the lack of feeling of obligation toward his parents.

There is a great need for a specialized program for parents confronted with the problems of rearing a brain-injured child. This program should help parents solve the day-to-day problems they face and should not be highly technical in content.

For the past eleven years, the staff of the Child Development Division of the Jewish Vocational Service in Milwaukee has been devoting its major energies to developing an evaluation, training, and counseling program for brain-injured children and their parents.

The evaluation effort has been directed toward (1) development of modifications of various psychological tests; (2) general experimental work with psychological tests to determine their potential use in evaluation; and (3) design of a number of brief tests to supplement the general psychological evaluation. Fifteen hundred children have been evaluated.

The training effort has been directed toward developing a specialized tutorial technique in perceptual and conceptual organization, relying principally on utilization of stimulus-response learning theories. Children are seen for forty-five-minute periods two or three times weekly, for an average eighteen-month span. Two hundred fifteen children have received this training.

The counseling effort has been directed toward development of techniques for use with parents of brain-injured children on an individual and group counseling basis. This effort focuses primarily upon the children's needs and the unique day-by-day problems encountered with a "misperceiving" organism. Two hundred ninety-five parents have been seen in groups, and 325 for individual counseling.

PROGRAM DEVELOPMENT

Seven years ago, a program of group discussions for mothers of children with organic damage was initiated. During the first three years, four programs were organized annually. Each group was composed of ten mothers; care was taken to match the groups in terms of chronological age and learning level of the child and socioeconomic status of the family. The groups met for thirty to thirty-six sessions during the school year from September to June.

Meetings were held at the same time each week, which enabled the mothers to maintain a fixed schedule in terms of baby-sitting and house-keeping arrangements. All mothers were between the ages of twenty-five and forty. None had a serious emotional problem that would detract from her potential to profit from the group experience.

A fee was charged for the group program on a three-semester basis. Fees were adjusted to the income level of each mother. Individual counseling was continually available for specific problems that could not be discussed in the group.

The past two years have witnessed a gradual expansion of the program. With the development of a preschool and nursery program for children, we have been able to establish a concurrent mother's discussion group related to each program of group services to children. In this manner, seven additional mothers' groups have been organized, with each group meeting weekly while the children are in nursery school. Two couples' groups of six each were also organized to meet on a biweekly basis during evening hours; one group comprised parents of adolescents. Both parents must attend each session.

Subsequent paragraphs describe a general approach that has been utilized with thirteen groups of parents during the past two years. All groups were composed of eight to twelve participants.

OBJECTIVES

This program was an attempt to provide a comfortable group setting where parents might meet regularly with a sympathetic and understanding professional to discuss their day-to-day problems concerning their children, and to learn from other parents. Additional objectives are

1. To constructively alter the parents' perception of the brain-injured child.

2. To teach parents principles for day-by-day identification, understanding, and guidance of the child's behavior.

3. To correct misconceptions, folk tales, and mystical beliefs regarding handicapped children.

4. To acquaint parents with present knowledge in the field of child growth and development.

5. To teach parents to recognize significant cues in their child's behaviorisms that are indicative of needs.

6. To teach them a systematic and consistent method of aiding development of organized response patterns in their child.

This counseling seeks to improve the parents' ability to deal effectively with the immediate problems in their lives, particularly in relation to their brain-injured child. The program is not designed to seek basic changes in the personality organizations of the mothers. No effort is made to uncover or probe. No encouragement is given to mothers to present problems that represent conflicts having no direct bearing upon their child.

In a sense, the leader protects the mothers from involving themselves unduly in their intrapsychic conflicts and rewards and reinforces their efforts to stay within the boundaries of the group objectives. If a mother in the group appears on the verge of "exposing" herself, the leader diverts the group tangentially. Although there is some griping among the mothers about the "head-in-the-sand attitudes" of their husbands, the discussion is kept at a level where no real secrets of the marital relationships are divulged. However, the counselor may invite the mother to an individual session to discuss a special problem.

ROLE OF THE COUNSELOR

The same counselor served all groups included in this report. During the early meetings of each group, he functioned on a direct basis, asking mothers to describe specific problem situations that previously had been discussed in individual counseling sessions. This was done to establish the "learning set" for the sessions.

Initially, this was a two-way conversation between the group leader and the mother whose problem had been selected. Within this conversation, the counselor drew in other mothers who were experiencing similar problems with their children. In each situation, he pointed out the misperceptions of the child, specific background-foreground problems, and tendencies to react to such irrelevant reactions as perseverative distractions.

The particular behavioral situation was discussed in the light of normal growth and development, and similarities and dissimilarities pointed out. The counselor asked the mother of the child under discussion and the group to define what they felt might be appropriate behavior in such a situation, and to delineate the specific skills and maturation comprising the elements of the situation. The counselor showed that behavioral configurations are made up of many different elements, and that failures of children in given situations may be traceable to their inability to cope with certain elements or their inability to organize their responses because of undeveloped skills.

After this learning situation, the group (initially, the counselor) worked out a possible approach to the problem that the reporting mother might attempt in improving the problem during the intervening week. The following week's session was devoted in part to this mother's report of her efforts in attempting the approach suggested.

This format became the pattern for all discussion periods with the counselor serving as moderator to move the group through the five steps: (1) reporting on a specific problem, (2) labeling the characteristics, (3) comparing to normal development and growth, (4) listing situational elements and skills, and (5) proposing a method to deal with the problem.

The initial directing, controlling, and organizing role of the counselor gradually changed to a more passive role as group interaction improved and as the mothers began to learn the process. This improved interaction permitted the counselor to be more sensitive to the group dynamics.

He injected comments into the group discussion whenever an emphasis or shift of emphasis seemed indicated, whenever a significant relationship needed to be pointed out, whenever a cue needed underlining, or whenever general background information on normal development or the theoretical thinking on brain injury could contribute to the discussion and expand the group's perception potential.

The counselor at all times kept the group at its work, analyzing their behavioral situations in terms of certain fixed principles and developing a solution that they, as parents, might attempt in the home situation. Involvement of the mother as an integrated and necessary part of the therapeutic effort to organize the child was continually pointed out.

During the course of the year, the mothers are taught the following principles:

1. The brain-injured child misperceives; his erratic and confusing behavior stems from these misperceptions. Recognizing his misperceptions is the first step toward understanding him.

2. Each failure of the child to conform or to see relationships becomes a challenge. If relationships and standards are made very simple, the child can conform. The problem becomes one of setting standards at such an easy level that the requirements are within the child's potential.

3. Simplicity becomes the key word in setting up behavior patterns for the child. Complicated routines or response patterns are achieved only gradually and then only when the various elements constituting the whole of a behavior pattern have been learned individually.

4. Each difficulty faced by the mother in relating to her child, or her child's relationship to his environment, may be analyzed in terms of components; a plan of development utilizing structured activity may be experimentally formulated to help the child.

5. The child cannot organize for himself; someone must do it for him. Once his living has been organized, he can gradually assume more and more responsibility for his own organization.

6. The child offers clues in his behavior that become warning signals of behavioral disorganization; the parents must become alerted to these clues in order to anticipate his needs.

7. An organized base is necessary before the child can advance to more complicated behaviors.

8. The parent is the chief organizer for the child because of the intensity of contact. Professional people help, but contact is too brief to effect total organization.

Experience with thirty-eight groups over a seven-year period has brought the following to light:

All parents start the group process at an *information-seeking* level. They want to ask questions and receive direct and specific answers. They want to know what to do, how to do it, and when.

This first stage gradually gives way to a *sharing* process in which they try to help each other by citing their own successes or failures and discuss each other's specific problems in terms of "Why don't you try this?"

This sharing stage, which operates specifically in the area of technique, gradually gives way to the *feeling* stage in which they help each other to examine their own feelings about their child's behavior, and to see how their own motivations, tensions, and attitudes are reflected in their child's behavior.

From this stage, they move into the *generalization* process in which they begin to consider the dynamics of child development and parental relationships for their other children as well.

The parents finally arrive at a *maturity* stage in which they integrate their brain-injured child into their total family unit and deal effectively with his problems because they understand the complexities of his development, and learn guiding principles to apply to their family relationships.

Through the group discussions, the parents learn how to set limits for their children and learn why limits are necessary. They learn how to prepare their children for new experiences. They learn how to set achievable standards for their children. The parents also learn how to reinforce positive constructive responses and to extinguish negative patterns.

Comparisons between the needs of normal children and brain-injured children are continuously pointed out by the group counselor as the parents discuss their problems.

The general therapeutic process is supportive and educative and aims at covering processes and reinforcing positive defense resources, rather than uncovering dynamics of conflict.

The daily problems of living with the brain-injured child create a stress upon a mother's normal defense structure and threaten her personality organization. If her defense structure enabled her to cope effectively with her family problems prior to this child, this becomes only a matter of developing her resources to cope with the additional pressure.

CONCLUSIONS

On the basis of this seven-year experiment in group counseling, several conclusions appear to be warranted:

1. A counseling technique to help parents develop experimental approaches to behavior organization in their brain-injured child is ego-strengthening, supportive, and practically helpful.

2. These parents experience a homogeneity of anxieties stemming from apprehension regarding the psychological and educational development of their children. Only on a secondary basis do they appear to concern themselves with factors in physical development.

3. A selection process in necessary to determine whether the needs of a particular parent might best be served in a group or individual counseling, setting, or whether referral for psychotherapy might be more profitable.

4. The parent of the brain-injured child must be considered an integral part of the organization of the child's behavior.

5. Parents can be taught to perceive their children differently and learn to deal with their children's problems more effectively.

6. Comments of the mothers consistently reflect changed response patterns in relation to problems represented by their children; they learn to apply a technique. There is some restoration of feelings of competency and self-worth.

7. The mothers learn to recognize their unique responsibility in developing organized response patterns in their children.

8. The number of mothers (10) selected for each group on an arbitrary basis has proven an effective and workable figure.

We feel that this technique has potentiality for effective counseling with parents of other types of child problems as well.

REFERENCE

1. Strauss, A. A., and Lehtinen, Laura E.: *The Other Child.* New York, Grune and Stratton, 1961.

Chapter 23

ABC'S FOR PARENTS
Aids to Management of the Slow Child at Home

MARYBETH P. FREY

Every handicapped child comes equipped with a set of parents. Any professional service for the child, whether public or private, group or individual, comes in contact with these parents. At this point the service can do one of three things: ignore the parents, give token service by telling the parents how their child is doing, or use the parents as valid observers who are capable of learning.

If we can accept the premise that the parent is a learner, then the professional worker needs to use every possible means of reaching the parent at his level of processing and learning. Supportive props may need to be used from time to time to reinforce the learning. The ABC's for parents could be used in this way.

These ABC's are not in any sequence of importance nor will every parent reach all these goals. They should be used as the needs and learning level of the parent indicate. Each item has inherent in it enough material for the parent to discuss and clarify for many sessions, but not every item will be comprehended, ingested, and utilized by every parent. Therefore, the ABC's could be used in part or in entirety on the basis of the parent's level of understanding of his child's problem and himself. These items can become the jumping-off place for professional and parent to begin to understand the child, the parent, and each other.—(Mrs.) Ruth Danks, Administrator, Child Development Center, Easter Seal Society of Milwaukee County.

A CCEPT your child's limitations without blame or resentment. However, seek understanding and do not resign yourself, or his future, to these limitations.

Reprinted from *Rehabilitation Literature*, Vol. 26 (1965), pp. 270-272. By permission of the author and publisher.

BUILD UP his confidence. He has a lesser, but still very important, potential to develop and contribute to life. Show him that you, too, have this confidence in spite of the fact that our world places much emphasis on mental facility.

COOPERATE with, rather than reject, special recommendations and programs advised by professionals who have studied your child's individual needs. (It is difficult for all of us to be objective when one of our own is involved.)

DIRECT his attention. Often the slow child appears to be less attentive and may require help in guiding concentration. If you recognize this problem, perhaps a little effort on your part could bring about improved listening, understanding, and response. One suggested method is to ask your child to come to you. Touch him lightly yet firmly (on shoulder, under chin, or take hand). Ask him to look directly at you. Explain that you are going to say something important. Add that you will expect him to repeat (statement), or to describe (action) when you finish. If this should be difficult for him at first, some patient prompting should help to establish habit.

EXPECT him to require more than the usual amount of time for almost everything (such as dressing, eating, chores, and homework). Not only is he more easily distracted, but physical slowness, including a possible lack of muscular coordination, will often accompany mental slowness. Make allowance for this extra time. Establish that tasks should be carried through to completion.

FORGET about unfair comparisons of school progress with that of children of friends, relatives, and neighbors and, likewise, of brothers and sisters. The slow child runs on his own track and at his own speed. He cannot be pushed until he is ready and able to pull. As an individual, he deserves to be treated as such and allowed to develop at his own rate and pattern.

GOVERN his discipline at home by that which is expected from his siblings. Permissiveness, through misguided sympathy, is not a kindness. It will cause him to be resented by his peers now, as well as cause him to be resentful toward you later when he must cope with rules of normal adult society. Be *consistent* in whatever disciplinary means you find most effective.

HELP him to take pride in doing those things he can do well. Find his own special talents and give genuine praise for effort and accomplishment in order that he experience success.

INSTITUTE a regular normal program of outside activities and cultural opportunities, or any extracurricular learning experiences, as a means of broadening his horizon. Don't deny him these by saying, "Oh, why bother. He won't get enough out of it anyway!" Suggested social experiences include church, Sunday school, museums, libraries, concerts, plays, sports, scouts, 4-H club, YMCA groups, summer camps, family vacations, community excursions, and a visit to observe farm or city living. If such opportunities are employed suitably, and in moderation, your child will be apt to surprise you. He could learn even more than you, and in a very different way. He is far more dependent upon various sensory perceptions and they serve him well on many such occasions. For instance, it's possible for a retarded child to describe a nature adventure by means of sights, smells, and sounds that we had missed completely.

JOHNNY usually can learn to read; also to do basic arithmetic, writing, and spelling—the four great essentials. True, the method may need to be examined and altered, or even to be tailor-made to fit. Your school will be glad to make recommendations for special help in academic areas if you will ask how you can help.

KEEP directions simple. The slow child does not assimilate as readily or remember as easily. Chain commands are apt to be confusing; both you and the child will be angry and frustrated at his failure to carry out the instructions. We've all been guilty of giving hurried, breathless directions like this: "Stop whatever you're doing, because I want you to run upstairs to the back bedroom and look in the top drawer of the tall chest and find my light blue thread and don't forget the door behind you and watch the stairs, too, but hurry because you can see that I'm waiting."

L ET the child set the pace in new learning situations at home. Watch carefully and constantly for signs of interest in a new undertaking and his first attempts to experiment. This is your clue to proceed quietly and promptly. Lend guidance to establishing certain limits as the activity may indicate, such as appropriate area and time, materials needed, proper use of tools, safety measures, personal strength, health, and endurance. This should give him courage and confidence in new undertakings.

M AKE certain that you stand ready to help him to solve his problems, but don't provide every answer. Mother but don't smother. To varying degrees he'll need nudges, reminders, gentle guidance, and perhaps some step-by-step organization of action or materials. Even in extreme situations try not to drop the last pieces of the jigsaw puzzle into place, thus diminishing his pride in task solution and completion.

N EVER give up hope for possible progress by wearily throwing in your sodden sponge. Give it (and your child) an extra squeeze, remembering that slower children don't always show the same level of ability in all branches of learning. In school, as well as at home, accomplishment in some subject areas forges ahead while in others it lags behind, possibly never leveling up. (Are *you* equally capable in mathematics, science, history, literature, and foreign languages?)

O PEN every possible door to his development and progress by finding, investigating, and considering all available persons and places specifically geared to aid your particular child. Often they cannot come to you; you must go to them.

PATIENCE and perseverance are recognized as personal attributes necessary to all parents. For guiding and training the slow learner these are even more important keynotes to improved harmony in the daily relationship. Positive or negative application of these attributes can result in observable changes. This child often has a shorter attention span and frequently a shorter retention span as well. Three R's useful for emphasizing in the home are repetition, retracing, and review, particularly when there has been some distraction or interruption in daily routine (as visitors, illness, and school absence). Great patience and perseverance are called for in establishing and maintaining general rapport.

QUIET CHILD? Beware! Such children may be calling out for help by their very silence. Don't assume that they are simply "good." Consider emotional problems, speech difficulties, and visual and auditory defects. (The regular physical check-ups should include eyes and ears.) Disabilities such as these can cause withdrawal from active participation and competition. However, at the other extreme, don't hover over your child watching for nonexistent defects when perhaps he is simply enjoying the child's private world we adults cannot penetrate. You'll need wisdom to know the difference!

REQUEST and read available material concerning your child's particular problems. Many experts, and agencies as well, stand ready to help you to gain new knowledge and understanding via the printed word in the comfort of your own home. Face up to facts, a child and his future may be dependent upon the parents' ability and willingness to read, react, and resolve.

SOCIAL acceptance is highly important to the slow learner's welfare outside the home situation. Without it he may well be shunned, belittled, ridiculed, dominated, and even exploited. Good training on your part as regards proper dress, health and hygiene, cleanliness and neatness, politeness and good manners, and general conduct in public surely will aid in bringing about acceptance. Any child, barring the lower custodial types, is capable of this learning with your encouragement. Thus the child will gain confidence in relationship to self and society. And you'll be proud of him, too!

TEACHING at home, whenever possible, should be concrete rather than abstract; deal in specifics and not in generalities. These are of prime importance for your slow-learner's best possible comprehension. Again, a reminder that he relies less on mental images and more on his senses, especially sight (visual patterns), touch (manipulation of objects), and auditory clues. Encourage his questions; ask questions of him. Guide him toward vocal and motoric expressions based on new learning experiences.

UNDERSTAND the importance that a familiar routine plays in the slower child's life. This is another facet of the constant repetitions he requires. Try to keep the main daily events as constant and consistent as your home schedule will allow. While *you* may be bored, remember that he likes to do most things at the same time, in the same place, and in the same way. Just knowing what to expect, when to expect it, where it will happen, and how to proceed gives this child a tremendous sense of needed security. For him, at least, monotony can breed content! To provide variety within this framework can be a real challenge to your ingenuity!

VERBALIZE as little as possible or, to put it simply, don't talk too much. Your child's verbal comprehension is slower and an excess of words is bound to result in mental confusion. Regardless of the type, or the importance of the conversation involved, he eventually "tunes us out." Meanwhile, we drone on much like an abandoned radio or TV!

Children learn to listen in many different ways and use both the eyes and ears in so doing. Examples include nonverbal direction (gestures only); sparse use of words but clues from facial expression, eye movements, or nods of head; and the actual pure auditory means whereby we "talk to the back of his head." Try this last with an inattentive child from time to time. Stand behind him and say, "I want you to listen to me now with just your ears—no peeking allowed." Note any improved ability to really concentrate without the availability of visual clues.

Watch your language, meaning your choice of words. Try, without actually "talking down" to him, to choose alternate words and phrases he will be able to understand more readily. Little by little, add others; his vocabulary will increase gradually and soon he will realize that certain terms mean the same thing. Do the same with words with opposite meanings. When there is a fairly good foundation in synonyms and antonyms, begin to help him make comparisons and to see relationships. Also, encourage your child to tell you a story, or to simply talk about any subject of his own choosing. Development of language skills will be a most useful tool to progress in all academic subjects.

X-ray your own state of mind. Let the light penetrate the darker corners. Then determine whether your attitudes, conscious or unconscious, might be further handicapping your child in his daily relationships at school, in the neighborhood, and even within the family. Resolve once again to pray for insight to see beyond his outward behavior to his inner feelings.

You will find that the slow child presents an ever-challenging personal problem to you as a parent. Whatever the hardships involved on your part, he is "affectionately yours." He has love to give if only you will accept it and return it in kind. You were chosen, among many others, as one able to provide the special thought and care that your child requires and deserves. Be adequate to that task in every way possible so that you may enjoy shared growth and progress, as well as understanding.

Zest for life and living must not be denied your slow learner. He, like all other human beings, wants and needs to "feel good about himself." Help him to realize that in our vast and complex world there is a need and a place for each of us. And, of course, *you* must believe in this yourself!

& We can't forget the ampersand, nor the quotation from the well-known author, Pearl S. Buck, who has experienced this problem first hand: "The test, I say again and again, of any civilization is the measure of consideration and care which it gives to its weakest members."

BIBLIOGRAPHY

Anderson, Camilla: *Jan, My Brain-Damaged Daughter.* Portland, Durham Press, 1963.

Ashlock, P.: *Teaching Reading to Individuals with Learning Difficulties.* Springfield, Thomas, 1966.

Barry, Hortense: *The Young Aphasic Child.* Washington, Volta Bureau, 1961.

Barsch, R.: *Achieving Perceptual-Motor Efficiency; A Space-Oriented Approach to Learning.* Seattle, Special Child, 1967.

Bateman, Barbara: *Learning Disabilities.* Seattle, Special Child Publications, 1971, Vol. 4.

Bateman, Barbara: *Temporal Learning.* San Raphael, Calif., Dimension, 1968.

Bender, Lauretta: *Psychopathology of Children with Organic Brain Disorders.* Springfield, Thomas, 1956.

Benyon, Sheila: *Intensive Programming for Slow Learners.* Columbus, C. E. Merrill, 1968.

Birch, Herbert George: *Brain Damage in Children; the Biological and Social Aspects.* Baltimore, Williams and Wilkins, 1964.

Bond, G. L., and Tinker, M. A.: *Reading Difficulties: Their Diagnosis and Correction.* New York, Appleton-Century-Crofts, 1957 (Rev. 1967).

Bortner, Morton: *Evaluation and Education of Children with Brain Damage.* Springfield, Thomas, 1967.

Brueckner, L. J., and Bond, G. L.: *The Diagnosis and Treatment of Learning Difficulties.* New York, Appleton-Century-Crofts, 1955.

Bush, Wilma Jo and Giles, Marian T.: *Aids to Psycholinguistic Teaching.* Columbus, C. E. Merrill, 1969.

Chaney, Clara C., and Kephart, Newell C.: *Motoric Aids to Learning.* Columbus, C. E. Merrill, 1968.

Clements, Sam D.: *Minimal Brain Dysfunction in Children.* U. S. Dept. HEW, 1966.

Cratty, Bryant J.: *Developmental Sequences of Perceptual-Motor Tasks.* Freeport, N. Y., Educational Activities, 1967.

Critchley, Macdonald: *Developmental Dyslexia.* London, Heinemann, 1964.

Cruickshank, W. (Ed.): *The Teacher of the Brain-Injured Child.* Syracuse, Syracuse Univ., 1966.

Cruickshank, W. M., Bontzen, F. A., Ratzegury, F. H., and Tannhauser, M. T.: *A Teaching Method for Brain-Injured and Hyperactive Children.* Syracuse, Syracuse Univ., 1961.

255

Delacato, Carl H.: *The Diagnosis and Treatment of Speech and Reading Problems.* Springfield, Thomas, 1965.

Early, George H.: *Perceptual Training in the Curriculum.* Columbus, C. E. Merrill, 1969.

Ebersole, M., Kephart, N. C., and Ebersole, J. B.: *Steps to Achievement for the Slow Learner.* Columbus, C. E. Merrill, 1968.

Ellingson, Careth: *The Shadow Children.* Chicago, Topaz Books, 1967.

Fernald, Grace M.: *Remedial Techniques in Basic Skill Subjects.* New York, McGraw-Hill, 1943.

Frierson, E. C., and Barbe, W. B.: *Educating Children with Learning Disabilities; Selected Readings.* New York, Appleton-Century-Crofts, 1967.

Gallagher, James: *A Comparison of Brain-Injured and Non-Brain-Injured Mentally Retarded Children.* Lafayette, Child Development, 1957.

Getman, G. N., and Kane, E. R.: *The Physiology of Readiness.* Minneapolis, Programs to Accelerate School Success, 1964.

Gillingham and Stillman: *Remedial Training for Children with Specific Disability in Reading, Spelling, and Penmanship.* Educator's Publishing Service, 1956.

Grzynkowicz, Wineva: *Teaching Inefficient Learners.* Springfield, Thomas, 1971.

Haring, N. G., and Phillips, E. L.: *Educating Emotionally Disturbed Children.* New York, McGraw-Hill, 1967.

Hegge, Thorleif G., Kirk, S. A., and Kirk, Winifred: *Remedial Reading Drills.* Ann Arbor, Wahr, 1940.

Hellmuth, Jerome: *Educational Therapy.* Seattle, Special Child Publications, 1966, Vol. 1.

Hellmuth, Jerome: *Learning Disorders.* Seattle, Special Child Publications, 1965, Vol. 1.

Hellmuth, Jerome: *Learning Disorders.* Seattle, Special Child Publications, 1966, Vol. 2.

Hellmuth, Jerome: *Learning Disorders.* Seattle, Special Child Publications, 1968, Vol. 3.

Hewett, F.: *The Emotionally Disturbed Child in the Classroom.* Boston, Allyn and Bacon, 1968.

Johnson, Doris J. and Myklebust, Helmer R.: *Learning Disabilities: Educational Principles and Practices.* New York, Grune and Stratton, 1967.

Kephart, N. C.: *Learning Disability: An Educational Adventure.* Lafayette, Kappa Delta Pi Press, 1968.

Kephart, N. C.: *The Slow Learner in the Classroom.* Columbus, C. E. Merrill, 1960, 1971.

McCarthy, James J., and Kirk, Samuel: *The Illinois Test of Psycholinguistic Abilities.* Rev. ed. Urbana, University of Illinois, 1968.

Mallison, Ruth: *Education as Therapy.* Seattle, Special Child, 1968.

Meeker, M. N.: *Structure of Intellect.* Columbus, C. E. Merrill, 1969.

Money, John (ed.): *Reading Disability: Progress and Research Needs in Dyslexia.* Baltimore, Johns Hopkins, 1962.

Monroe, G. E.: *Understanding Perceptual Differences.* Champaign, Stripes, 1967.

Myklebust, Helmer R.: *Progress in Learning Disabilities.* New York, Grune and Stratton, 1967, Vol. 1.

Rappaport, Sheldon: *Public Education for Children with Brain Dysfunction.* Syracuse, Syracuse Univ., 1969.

Roswell, Florence, and Natchez, Gladys: *Reading Disability: Diagnosis and Treatment.* New York, Basic Books, 1964.

Spache, G. D.: *Good Reading for Poor Readers.* Scarsdale, Garrard, 1966.

Segall, M., Campbell, D. T., and Herskovitx, M. J.: *The Influence of Culture on Visual Perception.* Indianapolis, Bobbs-Merrill, 1966.

Siegel, Ernest: *Helping the Brain Injured Child.* New York, Association for Brain Injured Children, 1961.

Stern, Catherine: *Children Discover Arithmetic: An Introduction to Structural Arithmetic.* New York, Harper, 1949.

Strauss, A. A., and Kephart, N. C.: *Psychopathology and Education of the Brain-Injured Child.* New York, Grune and Stratton, 1965, Vol. 2.

Strauss, A. A., and Lehtinen, Laura E.: *Psychopathology and Education of the Brain-Injured Child.* New York, Grune and Stratton, 1947, Vol. 1.

Thompson, Lloyd J.: *Reading Disability: Developmental Dyslexia.* Springfield, Thomas, 1966.

Valett, Robert E.: *The Remediation of Learning Disabilities.* Palo Alto, Fearon, 1968.

Waugh, Kenneth W., and Bush, Wilma Jo: *Diagnosing Learning Disorders.* Columbus, C. E. Merrill, 1971.

Young, M.: *Teaching Children with Special Learning Needs.* New York, John Day, 1967.